A W

O WISDOM
who camest out of the
mouth of the most high
reaching from end to
end mightily and
sweetly, come and teach
us the way of
PRUDENCE

EX
LIBRIS

PERSPECTIVE
FOR
RENEWAL

PERSPECTIVE
FOR
RENEWAL

By
Mary
Perkins
Ryan

THE LITURGICAL PRESS, COLLEGEVILLE, MINNESOTA

Contents

PERSPECTIVE
FOR
RENEWAL

CHAPTER 1

The Situation

Why we Catholics do not more effectively let our "light shine out to all who are in the house"—in view of our numbers, our zeal, our favorable situation in a uniquely pluralist society—is a continually recurring question. The touchy question of "leakage" is one phase of it and so is that of the dearth of Catholic intellectuals and artists. Another is our failure to make an impact on contemporary ways of thinking, acting and living, whether on the community level or in wider contexts. And the search for a satisfactory "spirituality for the laity" is still another.

Various historical, social, economic and psychological factors have been discussed in relation to this phenomenon. But there is a more basic cause that has seldom been mentioned: the very way in which the majority of American Catholics seem to picture the relationship between religion and life; between what they believe and what they do every day; between what they hope for as Christians and what they hope for as human beings; between their love of other people, their desire for affection and "belongingness," and what they think their faith tells them about the love of God and neighbor.

Our age is unique in the completeness of its orientation toward the use and enjoyment of new products of human activity. It is unique in its terrified fascination with what men are doing and may do. The Communist "mystique" of human work has its counterpart in our "mystique" of the secure and status-conferring job with its concomitant possessions. But the Catholic map of life, as most of us have been picturing it to ourselves, is laid out in a perspective that conceals, rather than reveals, the religious significance, the bearing, the implications of human activity and human achievement.

Our culture is unique both in its determination to believe that things are somehow getting better and better every day for everyone, and in its fear of the imminent destruction of civilization and all human life. People today are characterized by the peculiar urgency of their desire for "security," their irrational hope of securing a particular form of it, their unacknowledged fears that real security of any kind is no longer possible. Yet Christian hope, as most Catholics understand it, is irrelevant to these human hopes and fears; it refers only to the security of each individual "soul" after death.

People today are equally characterized by a peculiar sense of loneliness, of isolation in a world they do not understand. They are looking, in a new and urgent way, for affection and "belongingness" to give some stable starting-point from which to view and act in their world. Yet the love of God and neighbor inculcated by their faith, as most Catholics understand it, seems to take little cognizance of these needs.

To the priest or religious, this disconnection between religion and life may not, in a sense, seem to matter at all. If he thinks of all human concerns as ultimately frivolous and futile, he may even go about his work the more zealously. But the present apparent irrelevance of religion to life and of life to religion is fatal to the layman's carrying out of his Christian vocation. It means that he does not have one, except as a part-time job.

And this irrelevance is fatal to the full effectiveness of the work of the Church in our world, because so many of the Catholics who do take their religion seriously have a secular ideal of their own lives here and now, and of the life of their society. The advice which, as legend has it, was once given to the senior class in a great Catholic college: "Go out, my boys, and make every dollar you can, so long as it doesn't interfere with your spiritual life," may never have been given in so many words, but it is the ideal of lay life as too commonly understood. Obviously, such a point of view hardly leads to creative thinking and acting in the world.

Another perspective has been opening out in Catholic thought and life during the last decades—one in which faith and daily living, religion and human activities, the purpose of our individual lives and the purpose of history can be seen as one dynamic whole. This might be called the "perspective of the plan of salvation," since it orients each and all of us in relation to that plan. Or it might be called "the perspective of the Christian vocation," since it opens out the possibilities of that vocation in itself and as it can be carried out in every phase of Christian life.

The whole scope of this perspective is only just beginning to be caught sight of, its implications in the ways we think about and do things are just beginning to be sketched out and acted upon. Many people concerned with the special problems of the layman, therefore, have not yet realized that this perspective opens out a basic Christian "spirituality" which can provide the "spirituality for the laity" so much discussed and sought after today, while it would integrate and give added reality to the various specialized "spiritualities" of priests and religious.

Other people who are vitally interested in one or another aspect of this potential renewal have not as yet seen that this one aspect implies a whole way of looking at things. And many others regard one or another of these aspects with suspicion precisely because, behind their specific objections, they feel that such new departures do imply a whole new outlook, different from the one they have always accepted as "traditional." Not having any clear picture of what this outlook might be, they are afraid lest welcoming it would mean the loss of many cherished values and certainties.

There seems to be a need, therefore, to indicate the scope, the dimensions and implications of this outlook so that it can be seen as a whole—and to do so is the purpose of this essay. Such a brief sketch, however imperfect and inadequate, may serve to fill out and extend the vision of those already concerned with some aspect of the present renewal. It may reassure those who fear that it may prove to be merely another ivory-tower refuge for idealists or another "gimmick" for activists. And it may help to show those who are fearful of it that nothing they really value would be lost in such a reorientation of outlook, but rather much would be gained.

Obviously, such a reorientation, if it comes, must happen by a gradual process of leavening. It cannot be done simply by *fiats* from above. The Holy See has been giving mandates to promote many aspects of this reorientation ever since Leo XIII's pronouncements on the reconstruction of the social order, and great changes have already taken place. Yet it is still necessary to discover this outlook by means of considerable study and discussion. It is not yet being communicated generally in the living context of home, school, parish and general Catholic life—as it ultimately must be if it is to vitalize Catholic thinking and living. But this can only come about if those of us who do have, or see the necessity for making, opportunities for such study and discussion, ourselves grasp the scope and the implications of this outlook and try to realize them in our own lives.

This essay will, therefore, attempt first to present the main lines of this perspective as these begin to emerge in the course of reading some representative part of the available literature. Then it will indicate some of the implications that slowly become evident as one begins to think and act along these lines—implications affecting every aspect of thought and life, whether one be a priest, a religious or a layman. Next, it will point out how this perspective clarifies the roles of priest, religious and layman in carrying out the one Christian vocation in the whole life of the Church. And, finally, it will venture to indicate some of the reorientations in Catholic education and Catholic living that this outlook would seem to imply.

But first it seems necessary to delineate the basic pattern of the outlook still generally prevalent and the implications it has taken on in the mentality apparently characteristic of American Catholicism. Some of these implications, it is true, have already been rejected by many people. Yet they will never generally be rejected until they are seen as flowing from a mentality that continues to influence us all. And until we realize consciously the lines along which we have been thinking more or less unconsciously, we cannot carry out the reorientation toward another mentality which seems to be indicated today.

CHAPTER 2

The Present Perspective
and Its Implications

As the vast majority of American Catholics understand it, their faith teaches that the purpose of life on earth
is to achieve eternal happiness by dying in the state of grace,
the state in which they were placed at baptism. They are to
achieve this goal by believing the truths that God has revealed,
obeying the commandments of God, the commandments of the
Church and her moral teaching, and using the means of grace
—the Mass, sacraments, prayer, and other helps the Church
provides.

This summary follows the pattern: "My task in life
and how I am to achieve it," according to which Christian
doctrine has been taught for many generations, the pattern
laid out in most of the catechisms used since the seventeenth
century. As a *schema* for presenting the truths of the faith
in an orderly way for intellectual comprehension, this pattern
admirably serves its purpose. It is simple, clear, and even
appealing.

But this outline came into use at a time when the
age-old means of inculcating religious truth and religious
living through holy Scripture and the liturgy had fallen into
almost complete disuse. It soon came to provide the basis

for all religious instruction, and to do so in an increasingly secularized world. And so the originally vital concept that God has an eternal purpose for each of us and that He gives us in His love the means to attain it—a concept that elicits a heroic response when its real implications are grasped—has gradually come to be understood as meaning: "God has a task on earth for priests and religious: to provide truth, grace and guidance for the laity. But He has no task for the laity except to stay out of sin, to support those who provide these spiritual goods, and to get to heaven by using them." The answer to the question, "Why did God make you?" has come to mean, so far as the average layman is concerned:[1] "He made me to know Him through the answers in the catechisms I memorized when I was a child; to love and serve Him by obeying the moral law, going regularly to Mass and the sacraments, supporting the work of the Church with money and with personal effort when possible, saying my daily prayers— and so to get to heaven and be happy with Him forever."

But worse than such minimalizing, perhaps, is the fact that this outline, as it becomes part of our thinking, tends to be moulded by today's secular mentality into something like its own image.

The clergy and religious of the Church are thought of as the "professionals" and the "producers" in the field of

[1] That is, this is the idea of the layman's life held up as the practicable ideal by the majority of priests and religious, and, consequently, the idea actually held and lived by the more zealous and faithful of the laity. The most zealous make such additions as, for example, reading religious books and periodicals, attending study-clubs or classes, attending parish devotions and daily Mass, making a yearly mission or retreat.... The less zealous, of course, grow more and more vague in their notions of the Christian life, down to a kind of hope that if they go to Mass most Sundays, abstain from meat most Fridays, make their Easter duty and try, more or less, to keep the moral law, an understanding God will take care of them. And from this attitude it is not a great step to ceasing to bother at all about the obligations of the faith and so lapsing into complete indifference.

religion, entrusted with the task of providing, distributing and promoting the use of the various means to eternal security and happiness made available to mankind through the Church. Their work is concerned with the other-worldly, the sacred; the laity realize that priests and religious are, as it were, God's trusted assistants. And so they give them a respect of a quality quite different from that which they pay to those who serve any other of their needs. Yet this respect is colored by the professional-client, producer-consumer relationships to which they are accustomed in other aspects of life.[2]

The laity, of course, are to support this work of the Church so that they themselves will continue to have the spiritual care they need, and so that, through her missionaries, this care will be made available to everyone on earth. They are to support it with money, and by giving whatever time and energy they can spare to the activities of their parish, their diocese, and to other Catholic good works and organizations. They also indirectly aid in the work of the Church by bringing up those children whom they "give to God" to be the future priests, Sisters and Brothers of the Church, those who will carry on her works for future generations.

So the laity—the more zealous laity, that is—certainly feel associated with the work of the Church, but not as *their* work. They feel about it much as volunteer medical aids, fund-raisers for hospitals, contributors to funds for medical purposes feel about the work of doctors and regular medical personnel. Their role is to help the real professionals serve the community and the world.

Beyond this, every Catholic who is in the state of grace can help win grace for himself and for other people by offering all his prayers, works and sufferings to God in his daily morning offering. When he does so, explicitly or

---

[2] Neither clericalism nor anti-clericalism is peculiar to any age. Yet our particular American brand of clericalism, and the reaction to it, seems to have its own matter-of-fact, rather genial and business-like flavor.

implicitly, whatever he does or endures that is not positively sinful is transformed by the merits of Christ into a kind of spiritual currency, in return for which God will dispense His graces the more liberally—the rate of exchange, so to speak, being determined by his personal degree of grace.

From what seems to be the religious point of view, then, it makes no great difference what a lay Catholic does with his time and strength, his talents and opportunities, so long as he takes all the necessary precautions and means to stay in—or quickly return to—the state of grace, and so long as he does not explicitly retract his general intention of offering everything he does to God. He is to be applauded and assured of an extra heavenly reward for giving his spare time and money to helping the work of the Church. But it doesn't matter a great deal how he makes the money or spends the rest of his time, if he doesn't do anything explicitly and directly condemned by the moral teaching of the Church. In obeying this moral teaching, he has to fulfill the duties of his state in life, which include supporting his family if he has one. But it makes no difference supernaturally what kind of work he does—short of any thing clearly sinful—or how well he does it, if he manages to hold a job and so fulfill his duty of family support.

Thus the Catholic view of life has come to run parallel, as it were, to the modern secular view held by the enormous mass of men and women whose daily work holds no intrinsic interest for them—the commercial view which makes the primary purpose of any activity seem to be the gaining of some extrinsic wage, profit or benefit. Such workers put in their eight hours, not to accomplish something, but to make the money with which to pay for security and pleasure. And so Catholics presumably are to go through their lives to preserve spiritual security and to earn the grace needed to enjoy life everlasting.

The very theological definition of the essential joy of heaven as the "beatific vision" serves, in the modern context, to reinforce this parallelism. People are taught this definition from childhood without the inspired analogies of Scripture and the liturgy[3] to help them think about it, and therefore, if they think about it at all, they must make their own analogy from the life they know. As the weary worker, after his eight-hour day of routine toil, sits down in front of his TV set for rest and pleasure, so the Christian soul, after its earthly labors, will be rewarded with the passive enjoyment of a kind of heavenly TV that will keep him happy forever.

A man with the commercial outlook on his day's work may, of course, be toiling most unselfishly to earn security, pleasures and advantages for his family. In the same way, a Catholic may be going through a dull and wearing day's work and offering the merit of his actions for other people. But he does not think of the work itself as having any bearing on his or anyone else's eternal destiny.

Many Catholics, therefore, are only interested, as it were, in shorter hours and higher wages, on both the natural and supernatural levels. Others who are really interested in and committed to their work do it only for its own sake, like their fellow executives, scientists, technologists, without any idea that it might have some function in God's plan for mankind.

Even those who are working with zeal and conviction for some cause—to see that the hungry are fed, the sick healed, that social justice and decent conditions are ensured

----

[3] The sitting-on-a-cloud-and-playing-the-harp picture of heaven, derived (so far as the harp is concerned, at least) from the Apocalypse, would, of course, be no improvement. Here, and wherever the realities of God's love beyond our understanding and experience are concerned, we need all the "pictures" given in Scripture and the liturgy to see how each gives us a hint—and only a hint—of some aspect of what "it has not entered into the heart of man to conceive."

for one or another group—feel that what they are doing is God's will in some way, and that they are serving Christ in the people they are caring for; but they do not see how their working for this cause means that they are in any sense taking part in the redemptive work of Christ. Only the few who have full-time jobs in some form of "apostolate," therefore, feel that their working life and their religious life form one integral whole.

And this view, in turn, affects religious affairs. It does not seem to matter how well any activity that comes under the heading of "Catholic" carries out its intrinsic purposes, so long as carrying it out appears to be promoting spiritual security and the use of the means of grace. It doesn't matter how effectively (as to the psychology of the worshippers) Mass is celebrated or the sacraments administered, so long as the *ex opere operato* effect is assured and the faithful come to Mass and the sacraments regularly.

Catholic life has, certainly, gone on, even though conceived in these terms. Christ's truth has been imparted and received, even in the abstract capsule-forms to which it is so often reduced in catechisms and manuals. Christ's life is communicated in the sacraments, even though the recipients think of them in a more or less mechanical (or magical) framework. A great number of Catholics faithfully continue to attend Sunday Mass, even though a large proportion of them do so only to fulfill an obligation (or because to stay away would scandalize their families). Even though many zealous persons may think of holy Communion in utilitarian or sentimental terms, they do receive it, and in what often seem to be overwhelming numbers. Even though they think of the work of the Church as properly the work of priests and religious, by and large they support it with great generosity. The very success, in quantitative terms, which might seem to justify the present outlook, witnesses to the marvellous possibilities of fully Christian living which a more vital outlook might actualize.

Obviously, Catholic life as it is lived overflows in every direction the narrow limits of the outlook just described. Yet, this is the view of religion which continues to hold and mould many minds. It is the view taken for granted by vast numbers of zealous and less zealous American Catholics; it is that assumed in innumerable sermons, publications, pieces of "religious literature," in a great deal of vocational direction and counselling, in the promotion of religious "goods" and services.

It is this outlook which, it seems, is ultimately responsible—beneath the various sociological and economic causes—for the dearth of Catholic intellectuals and artists, for the continuation of the ghetto-mentality among so many groups, for our lack of positive impact on society.

And it is this outlook also which is responsible for a great deal of the indifference and "leakage," not only among those whose religious instruction has been received in weekly classes more or less faithfully attended, but also among those who have received their whole education under Catholic auspices. For no number of classes in religion or even in theology, given in the perspective of this outlook, can bring about the vital interweaving of faith and life needed to offset—without asking for miracles—the pull of "the lust of the flesh, the lust of the eyes, the pride of life." For some persons, certainly, fear of sin, fear of offending God, love of Christ and His holy Mother, are still strong enough motives to cause them to call on the help of grace in time of temptation. But for very many—and their number seems to be growing with alarming rapidity, especially among young people—it is otherwise.

For if religion seems only morally and sentimentally relevant to love and friendship, to the search for security, to the pursuit of a career, to the fear of failure, to all the absorbing interests of daily life, only the very simple and the very humble will be able to cling to God's law when they are suddenly faced with the necessity to make a real choice between the demands of faith and what seems to be "life."[4] If their understanding of their faith has not shown them the possibility of the dynamic polarization of life in all its aspects towards its Source and Goal, only the very few will be able to discover it for themselves.

And the present outlook, because of its impersonal and more or less mechanically moralistic qualities, seems to have little affinity for the hopeful tendencies of the present time: a sense of anguished responsibility for sharing intellectual and material goods with all mankind, a longing for real brotherhood and for personal intercommunication, a search for the Absolute.[5] None of these really come within its field of vision. And this is at least one reason why so many modern men of real good will do not even think of looking to the Church for the answers to the great questions life is asking of them—or, if they do look, fail to see that the life the Church offers contains the dynamic solutions they are seeking.

This is why it is important for us consciously to advert to the fact of this outlook, by which we are all unconsciously influenced to a greater or lesser extent. It is important to see what it implies and what practices in our Catholic life flow from it and continue to foster it. Otherwise we may, with the best intentions in the world, continue to hinder and frustrate the renewal already at work in the Church, even when we mean to further it. For—

4 Not to speak of the agonizing choice between a fairly healthy, normal and workable life, on the one hand, and an almost impossibly difficult one, on the other, frequently forced on married people under modern conditions by the moral law concerning artificial birth control.

5 See H. A. Balthasar, *Science, Religion and Christianity* (Westminster, Md.: Newman, 1958).

—To see everything only in the perspective of "my task in life... things I must do to achieve it" interferes with our realizing that everything flows from the initiative of God's infinite generosity, desiring to create a society of persons with whom to communicate as persons in the infinite riches of His own divine life of loving personal intercommunication.

—To see God's revelation of Himself and of His plan to re-establish all things in Christ merely as the collection of "truths I must believe" interferes with our seeing this revelation as His personal communication through His creative and re-creative Word—His communication to each of us as the persons we are and the persons He wants us to become in His Son, in the Spirit of love.

—To restrict God's self-donation to us in Christ through the sacraments to the order of "things I must do—use the means of grace" interferes with our coming to see the sacraments as acts of Christ incorporating us into the vital process of His death and resurrection in order to give us His glorious life in the Spirit.

—To limit our worship and prayer to the category of "means" to be used interferes with our coming to see them as our direct response to God's love offered through His Son with the very love He has given us—the love poured out in our hearts by the Holy Spirit.

—To think of the Church—the whole Church or our own parish church—only as a kind of supernatural filling-station interferes with our coming to see her as the Bride and Body of Christ, the royal and priestly People of God, to which we belong and to which all men are called to belong.

—To think of the clergy and religious of the Church as nothing but professional "producers" in the field of religion interferes with our beginning to see the scope and glory of the Christian vocation as such, and of the particular vocations of clergy, religious and laity.

—To think of our daily work and activity as merely passing the time of our years on earth in such a way as to stay out of sin and earn grace interferes with our coming to understand the humane, the social, and the historic dimensions of God's design, and of cooperating intelligently and wholeheartedly in carrying it out.

—To think of sin merely as something forbidden interferes with our coming to see the nature and scope of our struggle with our own fallen nature and with the "powers of this dark world." It interferes with our beginning to understand the scope of Christ's victory. It interferes with the full flowering of true Christian hope.

—To think of death as something to avoid thinking about, since it is so terrible and leads at best to the sufferings of purgatory, prevents our preparing for it as the climax of our Christian life, our sharing in the mystery of Christ's death so as to go with Him—even through the purifying fires of purgatory—to fullness of life in the Presence of God.

—To think of the Last Judgment only in a context of fear and trembling prevents our preparing and longing, humbly and hopefully, for Christ's return in glory to make the victory of God's loving mercy complete and visible, and to welcome all His own, body and soul, into the joy of their Lord.

—To think of the glorious life of the City of God, when He has made all things new and is finally all in all, as a disembodied existence of individualistic passive enjoyment interferes with our coming to see the dynamic scope of God's plan to restore all things in Christ, and giving ourselves fully and humanly to carrying it out.

—To think of the great commandments of love of God and neighbor as pious ways of stating the "thou shalt not's," to think of Christ's new command to love one another as He loves us as a counsel of perfection outside the scope of ordinary Catholic life, interferes with our coming to an understanding of the whole plan of God and striving effectively to carry out our part in it—to enable us, remade to the image of Christ and in Him, to live His own life of infinite generosity, the life of the Spirit.

Obviously, no reorientation, no renewal, is going to solve all problems. Even if everything in Catholic teaching and life were reordered along the lines of the perspective of the plan of salvation now emerging, it would not make all Catholics faithful and fervent, nor would it make all non-Catholics clamor for baptism. But it would confront Catholics with a real life—not merely a system of beliefs, prohibitions and practices, but the life given us by Christ in the Church— to accept and grow in, or to reject. It would give them a dynamic outlook, a spirituality to grow in and live by, if they choose to cooperate with Christ. And in so doing, it would present the gift of God to us in Christ, the life He offers to all men through the Church, at least a little less inadequately, so that they in turn could accept or reject it for what it is. Catholic life lived according to this outlook is not any easier, but it is Catholic and it is life.

CHAPTER 3

Perspective for Renewal

The perspective now beginning to emerge has, of course, always been present in authorized formulations of Catholic teaching—between the lines, as it were, of manuals and catechisms. The question is one of emphasis, not of doctrine. In God's providence, during the recent centuries in which this perspective has been latent rather than explicit, many aspects and values of the Christian life have been brought out and developed, aspects which can now be gathered up in a new and more vital synthesis.

Yet this new perspective is essentially that of sacred history itself. It is the perspective of the Fathers and of the *Summa Theologica* of St. Thomas: God creating all things by His Word, His Son, for the sake of sharing His love; that love pouring out through created things to be returned to Him in the praise all creation offers through the infinite praise of the Son; sin cutting off a part of creation from this current of love given and returned; God re-creating all things through His incarnate Word to gather them all once more, and more closely than in the first creation, into the current of His love.

It can be stated so simply that a child can begin to see things according to its basic pattern: "God made us to share good things with." As revealed and developed in Scripture, the liturgy, and Christian tradition, it opens out all the aspects of human life to the truth and love given us in Christ. It begins with God, not with man. But in so doing it shows each of us our place in the eternal "design of God's heart."

The wonderful "Good News" of Christianity to men of all times—but in a special way, perhaps, to us today—is that God, the infinitely Other, the Absolute and All-holy, is not Abstraction, is not Isolation, but is infinite personal self-giving, in the inner life of the Father with the Son in the Spirit, and in the making and remaking of all things. The ultimate reality is to be found, not in infinite Aloneness, but in the presence of the divine Persons to one another, in their dynamic "communication"[1] in perfect unity. The final meaning of everything—of our own existence, of all human history—is to be found where we would most deeply desire that it might be found: in our being brought together, in the perfected reality of what we are and of what we are to one another, into this very presence and communication.

God calls each of us into existence as a person and re-creates us as "sons in the Son" so that we may share in the very current of the Son's communication with the Father in the Spirit. God calls us into existence as members of human society and re-creates us as members of the society of the Church so that His own communicativeness may flow in us and through us, so that as a society of persons we may be brought into the very "society" of the Most Holy Trinity. God calls us into existence as *human* persons, psycho-physical persons, bound up with material reality in our coming-to-be,

---

1 "Communication" seems the most meaningful word one can use today, since its many analogous uses all imply a mutual sharing by persons, a sharing in and sharing of "good things"— information, material goods, truth and love, the deepest realities of personality. Of course, we can only apply this word analogously to the inner life of the Most Holy Trinity, realizing that this life is the supreme analogue of all true "communication" in every order.

in our being and our acting, so that material creation too, through us, may be a medium and a means of our communicating with God and with one another, so that it may be gathered up, through us, into the eternal praise that the Son offers to the Father in the love of the Spirit.

But to be a created person means to be capable of opening oneself out to, or of closing oneself against, the self-giving of another, the self-giving of God. It means to be capable of accepting and throwing oneself into the current of God's infinite generosity, or to choose to be locked up in one's own self.

Our first parents made this choice of themselves in preference to God, following the lead of the Evil One, the first and greatest creature to refuse God's love. Their sin brought death into the world, since it meant the refusal of God's own life. It brought isolation and disunity, since it meant the refusal of unifying love. It brought slavery to the forces of death and disunity. In refusing the possibility of loving God with His own love, man became enslaved to himself. The whole drive of his being, designed to open out to the infinite freedom of God's love, turned back upon itself and tended to enslave to its own uses other men and material things. In refusing the service of God which is freedom, man became enslaved, not only to himself and to other men, but to the Evil One and to his purpose—to keep men away from their true good, from God.

The design of God's mercy, which He has been carrying out through the developing stages of human history, is, then, to free us from this slavery, to overcome this death, to do away with the obstacles to the free flowing of His love to us and through us, to bring us together in unity into His life and happiness. It is to re-create us to the image of His Son in the Spirit of love, so that we all may become the persons with whom He desires to communicate for all eternity in His Son, in a society permeated and transfigured by the

Spirit, through which God's love will flow in perfect freedom and joy, in a world itself become a perfect medium of communication and praise.

And God carries out this design precisely *by* communicating with men, by being present and acting in our midst in progressively greater intimacy in each stage of His design, until, when human history has ended, God will be "all in all."

During the centuries of the Old Testament, God "spoke in many ways and diverse manners to our fathers through the prophets." God's Word expressed itself in human language—the language of events and actions, of His wonderful works, of human reactions and ideas, finally set down in human words.[2] By this Word, God called and formed one people as His own; He was present among them. In His dealings with that people, He prepared for, promised, and foreshadowed the call of all mankind in Christ. He promised that in the times of the Redeemer to come, He would be present among His people, He would speak to them in a new and more perfect way. He would pour out His own Spirit into their hearts, so that they could truly be His own, truly respond to His love in worship and in life.

Then, in the fullness of time, God spoke to men, He became present among men, in His Son-made-man. The Word was made flesh and dwelt amongst us, the Word who is the Only-begotten of the Father. And in Christ, man could at last respond adequately to God's love, in the human nature, wholly obedient to the Spirit, which the Son of God had united to Himself.

Now, through all the centuries until the end of time, God communicates with men, God is present among men, through Christ present and active in the Church, not in one

___

[2] See H. A. Balthasar, "God has Spoken in Human Language," in *The Liturgy and the Word of God* (Collegeville, Minn.: Liturgical Press, 1959).

place alone, but all over the world. Through those empowered to speak and act in His Name and with His power, Christ communicates His Father's message, He communicates His life and His Spirit, in which we can truly call God "Father," in which we can respond to Him, in worship and in life, with Christ's own response. And through the Church—through us—Christ continues to carry out God's design of drawing all things to Himself, of re-establishing all things in Himself in whom God's communication with man and man's communication with God form one dynamic unity in the Spirit of love.[3] When this work is completed, then human history will have achieved its purpose. Christ will return in glory to inaugurate the perfect life of the City of God, in which God will be all in all.

Thus, in each stage of the plan of salvation God remakes men according to the design of His heart by dealing with them as persons, and as the human persons they are. By speaking to us in human language, by acting among us through His own Son-made-man, through the human messengers in whom His Son speaks and acts, He awakens us as persons to communication with Him. He awakens us to receive as free persons the Spirit of love and true freedom, in whom we can live and act and pray as "sons in the Son." He awakens us to share, if we will, in carrying out His design, to become co-workers with Christ, so that for all eternity we may rejoice in the fulfillment of this design, entirely the work of God's mercy, and yet also our work.

And so we see another dimension of God's generosity. He puts us in the amazing position, as it were, of being able to give to Him. God who made us without our consent

---

[3] "In Jesus Christ is fulfilled the word as a distinct being; as a dynamic creative entity; as that which gives form and intelligibility to the reality which it signifies; as the self-revelation of God; as a point of personal encounter between God and man." John L. McKenzie, S.J., "The Word of God in the Old Testament," *Theological Studies*, June, 1960.

does not save us without it precisely because to be "saved" means to be willing to be reoriented by the Spirit to free self-giving to other human persons and to God. It means to open oneself out to, to throw oneself into, the current of God's own self-giving, God's love.

This is why the love of God and neighbor are the two great commandments, summing up the whole Law and the prophets. These two commandments orient us precisely toward the very purpose of our creation and re-creation: fully personal communication with God, and communication with one another in God's love.

But Christ's new command is to love one another as He loved us, even to laying down His life. And this is because, in the human situation as it has been made by sin, laying down our lives is the only way of loving with God's own love. Because of sin, we have to "die daily" in any case—the minor deaths of pain, weariness, frustration, and, finally, physical death itself. But because of Christ, with Him and in Him, our daily dying and our physical death can become the means of loving God and of carrying out His plan to restore all things in Christ.

In becoming man, the Son of God took on Himself the whole burden of the human situation. He became "like us in all things save sin." His eternal communication with the Father was to be expressed in human terms, in a human life. And, in the human situation of refusal of God's love, the situation of death, isolation and enslavement to evil, this meant obedience unto death, even the death of the Cross. It was by freely undergoing, for love of His Father and of us, all the effects of human sins that Christ broke through, as it were, the barriers that sin and the Evil One had set up against the communication of God's life and love to men. It was by dying that He destroyed our death. By dying He overcame the Evil One, the enemy of God and mankind. He burst open the gates of death's prison-house, He set mankind free from slavery to sin and from the fear of death.

And by rising again, He restored our life. By going through death to the glory of His risen life at the right hand of the Father, He remade the path of human life, so that for those who would follow Him, it would no longer end in the darkness of death, but would lead through death to full and everlasting light and life. Or, better, He made Himself the *way* by which men might go with Him through human life and death to the life and glory that God desires to share with them.

In Him, "the substance of our frail human nature which He had united with Himself" lives forever at the right hand of the Father. In Him, our human nature is fully charged and transfigured by the Spirit.[4] The Lord who suffered and died as we do has been made the source of true life to all who will believe in Him, bringing back all things in Himself into the living unity of God's love.

God's design is thus already perfectly achieved in Christ Himself, or, better, it is Christ. It is perfectly achieved

---

[4] In the language of holy Scripture, "spirit" is what makes any living thing *alive* (the Hebrew word, like the Greek and Latin, is derived from a root meaning "breath," the most evident sign of life). The Spirit, the Spirit of God, is infinite life, vitality, creativeness, freedom, love. Hence "spirit" is not opposed to matter as the immaterial to the material. "Spirit" is opposed to "the flesh," that is, to the limitations, the less-aliveness of human nature in the weakness of its actual condition. The Word was made flesh, He took upon Himself this weakness, "like us in all things save sin," to bring our *whole* human nature, body and soul, into the life of the Spirit. The "spiritual man" is thus the whole man as God means him to be, the man who has "passed over" with Christ to the fullness of true human life, the life of the risen Christ, so far as is possible on this earth, anticipating and hastening toward the full transfiguration of the resurrection. And the "spiritual life" is a fully human life, oriented towards the carrying out of God's design thus to make us fully alive in Christ.

in His Mother, the new Eve, the human person who perfectly cooperated in His work, exemplar of redeemed mankind. She already shares, body and soul, in the glory of her Son and in His communicating of God's redeeming love.

God's design is already achieved, though not yet perfectly, in the holy ones in heaven, who communicate with God in the joy of perfect praise, though not as yet in the integrity of glorified human nature, in the complete joy of the whole perfected City of God. God's design is also already achieved, in a sense, in the holy souls still undergoing the purification of purgatory.

God's design is already achieved also in the members of the Church here on earth inasmuch as, here and now, we are communicating with God through His Word in the Spirit, and communicating with one another in the assembly of the Church, formed and animated by the Spirit. Our communicating with Him and with one another in Him here on earth is according to the mode of faith and hope, not vision and pure joy, but it is real communication nonetheless.

We receive the Word of God, revealing Himself and His plan, inviting our response and cooperation, in all Christian teaching, but in a special and direct way in the inspired words of holy Scripture, interpreted by the tradition of the Church and "proclaimed" to us in the Church, above all in her liturgy.[5]

---

[5] The Word of holy Scripture is formally proclaimed to the assembled people of God in the Readings (Lesson, Epistle, Gospel) of the Mass, assigned by the "teaching Church" and given by the mouth of her appointed representative. The Word of Scripture is also "proclaimed," in a wider sense, in and by the whole liturgy, which is formed by it and of which it forms the basic texture, so to say. In so doing, the liturgy brings out the threefold relevance of Scripture to us: as opening out the meaning of the liturgical celebration as the continuation here and now, in the sacramental mode suited to these "last times," of the wonderful works of God in the Old Testament and the New; as opening out our Christian vocation; as opening out the fulfillment of all figures, the ultimate reality of all sacraments, the purpose of all human life and history, in the life of the world to come.

And we receive this re-creative Word, which is Christ Himself, in the sacraments, incorporating us into the very process of His death and resurrection and giving us His Spirit, so that we may die to the old life of isolation and slavery, and be reborn and grow in His life of freedom and love.

We respond to God in and through His Word by the worship "in spirit and in truth" that the Church and her members offer to the Father through Christ: the worship of the Eucharistic Sacrifice, in which we join in Christ's great act of response to His Father's love, in His work of redemption made present in our midst; Christian prayer formed by the Word of God and offered through Christ; Christian living, our "spiritual service."

But God's design is not yet fully carried out in us. In thus communicating with God in and through Christ in the Church here on earth, we are being formed by the Spirit more and more completely into one Body, one intercommunicating holy society. We are still being redeemed from the old life in order to live Christ's life. We are still on the way to becoming fully the persons He means us to be, the persons with whom He wishes to communicate for all eternity, the persons whose intercommunication with one another is to contribute to the eternal delight of the City of God. In all His communicating with us here on earth, He is calling into existence, re-forming and re-creating the "new men," remade as their true selves in the life of the Spirit, who all together will make up the perfect society of the City of God, one perfect Man in Christ.

And God's design is not yet fully carried out in human history. Present in His Church until the end of time, Christ proclaims God's message and extends His invitation to all men. He gathers those who welcome His message with faith into the society of the Church, His Bride, His Body, which is thus becoming, as it were, His completion, "the fullness of Him who is wholly fulfilled in all."

Here, therefore, is the glory of the Christian vocation on earth: to communicate with Christ in a way foreshadowed in deep human friendships and symbolized by
human marriage, by sharing, intentionally and willingly, in
His praise of the Father and His work for men. All men
are called to this vocation. All who truly seek to be enlightened by God receive in some way the Light that enlightens every man. All who seek to serve God and their
neighbor are, in fact, cooperating in Christ's work ("Lord,
when did we see Thee..."). But we who believe in Christ
and are incorporated into His life by baptism know by faith
that in His mercy He has chosen us to be aware and responsible instruments of His love.

The bishops and their collaborators, the priests of
the Church, have been given a unique share in this work.
They speak in Christ's Name, they act in His very Person
so as to make His word, His redeeming acts, His sacrifice,
and the guidance of His Spirit present on earth through the
ages.

But all the members of the Church, by the very
fact that they are receiving this communicative Word of life
which is Christ, by the fact that the Spirit has been poured
out upon them, are called to cooperate with Christ in com-
pleting and extending the work of God's love in themselves
and in the world.

We do not know in what ways God's invitation to
share His life reaches those who never effectively hear His
Word proclaimed through the Church. But we do know our
responsibility to proclaim that Word to other people, according
to our various vocations, by words and by our lives and
actions. And we know our responsibility to make it less difficult for all our brothers on earth effectively to hear and
respond to God's invitation, however it may reach them.

God's design to restore all things in Christ is not
being carried out in a vacuum, but in the developing concrete

human situation from age to age. Throughout history God continues to bring into existence and to give men all the good things of creation—their lives, their human capabilities, material things. As all these created things themselves declare the glory of God, so they are meant to be means of our communicating with Him. They are meant to be material for our appreciative praise of His wisdom and power and beauty, shown in His handiwork itself and made perceptible in new ways by human art and by human achievement. And they are designed also to be the means whereby men help one another to develop their human personalities in a human society, itself developing into the fullness of communication with God and intercommunication among men.

But, because of the Fall, even as God gives these gifts to men, they become in some way "enslaved to corruption." We can far more easily use our lives, our powers, and material things as instruments of selfishness, disunity, distraction, than as instruments of communication and life. The "powers of this dark world" make use of our ignorance, weakness, selfishness and sinfulness, and of God's gifts to keep men from hearing God's message and returning to His love, and from helping one another to the fullness of human life.

Our cooperation with God's design in ourselves and in the world must, therefore, mean cooperating simultaneously, as it were, in His work of creation, and in His work of redemption and re-creation. As we receive our existence, our developing powers, our opportunities and material things, we have to struggle to wrest them from the service of the Enemy and of our own selfishness, and to restore them to the service of God's creative and re-creative love, to the service of our neighbor in that love.

Christ has conquered the Enemy, but His victory has to be completed in us and in the world, as our own lives and human history unfold. We share in that victory even now by our faith in Christ and by our incorporation into

His life. And since the life He gives us is the life of the Spirit, freedom to love as Christ loves, we are to live that life here on earth by sharing in His own suffering and struggle to free men from slavery to evil, to communicate God's life and love.

Our own death will be the climax and conclusion of this struggle for each of us individually. If, by God's mercy, we have given over our essential freedom to Christ's life in us, then we shall go with Him through death to the fullness of true life—life with Christ and His saints in the presence of the Father. The more completely that we have already died to any life other than Christ's before death comes to us, the more our death will be, like His and in His, a free-will offering of love to the Father, and the more quickly we shall be admitted into the joy of His presence.

But the mysterious and imperceptible carrying-out of God's plan through the struggle and confusion of human history will go on until Christ returns in glory to judge the living and the dead—that is, to disclose openly to all men the judgment that each has already pronounced on himself by accepting the Light or refusing it. Then, and not until then, will the victory be complete, the meaning of history unfolded. Then the full, true and eternal life of all those who have accepted God's love will begin, in the City of God in which He will be all in all.

The focus of the Christian life is, therefore, a communicating with God which includes of its very nature communicating with our fellow-men, here and hereafter. The Christian life is oriented upward to a communication with God in the community of the Church, which draws into its current our own lives and actions and the material things we deal with, and, in some sense, the human groups and societies of which we are a part. And the Christian life is oriented forward to the carrying-out and completion of God's plan in the perfect "communicating"—in which the new heaven and earth will share—of the City of God hereafter.

In such a perspective, obviously, all human life and activity are seen as potentially religious and, therefore, meaningful, in the sense of being capable of being drawn into the current of God's communicating and redeeming love. Seeing things in this way does not make people more "pious," in the present sentimental meaning of the word. Nor does it make them more "religious," in the sense of living according to a static, externally religious pattern of life imposed by authority, social pressure, or custom. But a mentality formed along these lines does focus all life and activity dynamically toward the supreme object of faith: the love of God revealed and given to us in Christ our Lord, and toward communication in and of that love.

In this perspective also, the human search for security and happiness, for experience and "the good life," can be realistically evaluated, and, equally, the mystery of suffering seen in its true light. It becomes clear that the necessity to lose one's life in order to save it is not a pious metaphor, but literal fact. For everything human, including the most legitimate human aspirations, must be reoriented, by the power of Christ's saving death, through our dying in Him to the "old life" of self-limiting selfishness to live in the freedom of the life of the Spirit. And the perfect life, the life of personal and social joy in God and in one another which is the final purpose of our creation and re-creation, will only be achieved when, at Christ's return in glory, the old order completely passes away and God "makes all things new."

But one aspect of Christian love is to see to it that our fellowmen have, so to say, a life to lose. That is, we must strive, under the conditions of the present order, to see to it that the conditions of human living are such that every man can, if he will, become aware of his own freedom and so freely choose to lay down his own life in the service of love—which means in the service of Christ, whether he recognizes Him or not. And such striving must, in fact, be ordered toward a fully human "good life" for all men.

In this perspective also, all our human affections find their reality and their true orientation. The love between husband and wife that married people, at best, only strive toward, the tried love of true friends for one another, are found to be images and analogues of the love between Christ and the Church, the love possible between Christ and each of us. The love that is pictured as always existing and that sometimes does exist in fact between parents and children is found to be the image and analogue of the love between the Father and His Son, the love that He has for us whom He has adopted in His Son, and that which He allows and enables us to have for Him.

But it becomes clear that all human loves are only true to their own nature and true analogues of divine realities when, by the power of the Spirit, they have reoriented from ingrowing self-centeredness and opened out to the current of God's own love. And our desire for "community" is fully explained in this light, since true community, beyond thought or hope, is precisely what God has made us and is remaking us for.

In this perspective, then, the "intellectual" can find the true bearing and significance of his quest and his work: to discover and to make known to others some reflection of infinite Wisdom, so that he himself and his fellow men may the more fully appreciate and praise God for His wonderful works in creation and re-creation and may enter the more fully into the design of His love. The artist can find the true context, the fruitful purpose of his striving and his making: to perceive the wonder of God's making and remaking and to make this wonder shine out in his own work, which thus becomes in a special way his praise of God and the cause of others' praise. And the man of action here finds the ultimate significance and purpose of getting anything done here on earth: "Inasmuch as you have done this to one of My least brethren...."

Priests and religious may, therefore, discover in this perspective an integration and a realism perhaps hitherto only implicit in the particular spiritualities by which they have been living. And the layman finds in it the spirituality he has been looking for—one that can be lived out in his own life, whatever his particular work and circumstances, one that gives meaning and direction to its every aspect, one that unites him, not in spite of his daily life and activity, but by means of it, with God and with his fellow men.

As things are, this way of looking at the Christian life is not the way generally communicated to Catholics in the ordinary course of their education and Catholic practice. It must be more or less effortfully acquired by study, though it is essentially so simple and integral, the story of God's love for men. But, obviously, it is far more than a way of looking at life; it implies a way of living. Before considering how it might be generally communicated to Catholics in the ordinary course of their Catholic life, therefore, we need to consider what practical implications this outlook may take on in the life of someone—priest, religious or layman—who is discovering it and trying to think and act in accordance with it.

CHAPTER 4

Orientation to Faith and Reality

As the perspective so sketchily indicated in the previous chapter begins to open out, the discoverer may realize that to see things in this way is going to give a new tonality to life as well as a new orientation. It will involve living a life which is much more directly and intensely a life of faith than that demanded by the "things I must believe and do" mentality.

Formerly, he could concentrate on those aspects of revealed truth which seemed most "reasonable." Now he is being oriented toward the supreme object of faith: the love of God given us in Christ. The lines of this perspective all converge, not in ourselves and our interests, but in what St. Paul calls "the mystery of Christ." They converge beyond all human concerns in the transcendent "Other," who yet speaks to us through His Son-made-man in human words and through human acts.

This way of looking at things directs attention precisely to the design of God's wisdom which seems folly to the human wisdom of every age. And in so doing it emphasizes what the other mentality allows one virtually to ignore: the fact of the Fall, the power of the Enemy, the redeeming death of Christ, the necessity of dying with Him in order to live, the return of Christ to inaugurate the final victory of our resurrection with Him.

But it is not so much this new demand for faith which, perhaps, may strike the discoverer as strange and initially repellent; it is, rather, what might be called the "realism" of this outlook. There is something which at first seems uncalled for, not quite decent, and even rather frightening, in agreeing to be put in touch with reality, not apart from faith, but in and through faith.

Formerly, he realizes, he had been left to derive his own ideas of God, of Christ, of his own relationship with Him, from abstract definitions, human representations, and his own intuitions. Now he begins with awe to find God revealing who He is and what He wants his relationship with Him to be—revealing this through His inspired Word communicated in the life of the Church. And, at the same time, he discovers that God really knows who and what he is, that He deals with men through Christ in the Church as human beings—as the human persons they are—not as minds or "souls"—to make them into the complete "christ-ened" persons He wants each to become. And he realizes that God wants us to communicate with Him as ourselves, to open out to Him every aspect of the selves we are, so that His truth and love may wholly permeate and re-create us.

This realism may begin to open out in the idea and experience of true internal and external participation in the liturgy, above all in the holy Sacrifice: to the priest, in the realization that all the members of his congregation actually have a part in "his" Mass; to the religious who is not a priest and to the layman, in the realization that he himself does have such a part. At the center and heart of our Christian life on earth, God does not want His people to be merely "souls" passively receiving grace produced by the sacred rites; He wants all Christians actively to receive and to respond to His communication and self-giving in Christ and to do so as fully human persons assembled in the community of the Church.

And the discovery of God's realism in dealing with us continues with the opening out of holy Scripture received in the tradition of the Church, above all in the liturgy. As the discoverer begins to realize that Scripture is not a rather vague, if inspired and poetic, way of telling us truths that have since been put more neatly into dogmatic formulas, but the Word of God speaking to us in the way He wants us to hear Him and the Word God gives us to speak to Him with— then liturgy, prayer, and life all begin to take on new dimensions. As he begins to "hear" holy Scripture in this way, as he begins to pray the psalms, understood in the context of the liturgy, as his own prayers, he finds that this language, which at first may have seemed so strange, is the native speech of our human nature used by God to form us to the likeness of His incarnate Son.

And so he discovers that God has something to say to him personally, something that calls for a total response and a total commitment. For God's communication with us in the Church reveals Himself, but in revealing Himself in Christ, He reveals the design of His mercy to unite us all with Himself in Christ. He invites us to take our part in carrying out that design, He incorporates us into its dynamic realization in history, He enables us always to take part in it more fully.

And our response to God, formed by His Word and offered through Christ, is, above all, praise[1] of the Most Holy as He reveals and gives Himself to us in Christ, a praise that of its nature includes our self-offering to the design of God's merciful love to be carried out, according to the Father's will, in ourselves and in the whole world.

In this way the discoverer begins to appreciate the all-inclusive realism of the Christian spiritual life. He begins

---

[1] Christian praise includes all the modes of Christian prayer: "confessing" God's majesty by adoration, His goodness by thanksgiving, His mercy by asking for mercy, His kindness and mercy by trustfully asking for what we need.

to see that it is not meant to be an incorporeal, "unearthly" life, but one that engages our whole selves, permeates all that we are and do. Obviously, the focus of this life must be prayer, a prayer centered in "hearing" the Word of God in faith and responding to Him with a prayer formed by and offered through that Word.[2] But such a prayer will be meaningless unless he allows God's Word to purify and reorder his whole life, unless he cooperates with the work of the Spirit in ordering himself and his activities toward carrying out God's design in himself and in the world.

SELF-DEVELOPMENT IN THE SERVICE OF LOVE

Here the discoverer begins to realize that the intuitions both of modern humanism and of modern psychology echo, in different modes, the perennial Christian message. True humanism has always been concerned to show that "becoming oneself" is a difficult and arduous task, the work of a lifetime of self-development and self-discipline. And modern

[2] The question of reorienting and developing one's prayer-life along these lines (and of its potential flowering into contemplative prayer strictly so called), for the priest, the religious and the layman, is expertly and realistically handled by Louis Bouyer in Introduction to the Spiritual Life (New York: Desclee).

A simple and practical way for the layman might be: some study, however brief, of the texts of each Sunday's (or day's) Mass, as illuminated by the context of the whole Mass and the liturgical season, and by their context in holy Scripture; then the prayerful reading of one or more of these texts as God's Word to him here and now, leading into a response to God's communication with one or more of the chants and prayers of the same Mass, opening out into a prayer thus formed by God's Word, a prayer of self-commitment with Christ to the demands indicated by that Word.

Such a form of "meditation" would form the core of his daily prayer, ordered toward participation in the holy Sacrifice. It could be expanded by the use of one or more "Hours" as found in one of the various breviaries, as circumstances allow, or by recalling now and then one of the phrases of the texts

psychology has discovered existentially, as it were, that the attainment of true human maturity takes place, when it does, not only through the balanced development and exercise of one's powers, but through a series of more or less painful "dyings" to the securities and satisfactions of one stage of life in order to reach another and a higher stage. The person who is able thus to "die" to childhood, to adolescence, to young adulthood, in due order, is opened out from his initial self-absorption to the freedom to love outside himself, to love intelligently and unselfishly, for the sake of the persons loved. And this is what true self-fulfillment and maturity consist in.

Thus our human task of developing and disciplining our human powers for the sake of communication with God and with our fellow men can take over and transfigure the human task of "becoming oneself" with all that this implies. The realization of this possibility gives a new incentive and orientation to all "humanistic" efforts to develop one's appreciative and communicative powers. One finds that one does not only "owe it to oneself" to take and make the opportunities for spiritual, mental and emotional growth, for cul-

he has meditated on and prayed, by connecting it with praying the Rosary, etc.

The prayerful study of the missal texts will probably indicate the need and the possibility of some wider study of holy Scripture and the liturgy, as his circumstances allow. Many missals offer some aids to the Christian understanding of the texts; commentaries and books along these lines are beginning to be available on a popular level.

We are singularly blessed today in that the efforts of so much modern scholarship are being devoted to opening out the Scriptures precisely as "communication"—divine communication carried out through many kinds of human communication, the divine Word incarnating itself so thoroughly in human language and human history that the more fully one appreciates the mentality and the mode of expression of its human messengers, the more fully one can receive its message—given the essential, which is opening oneself out to the Spirit who guides the Church in her understanding of holy Scripture and in her prayer, and following that guidance as it is given to us in the tradition of the Church, concentrated, as it were, in the liturgy.

tural development, for mental and physical health, that fit into the context of one's particular vocation and the demands of charity; one owes all this to God and to neighbor and to true love of self, in order to become a better instrument of praise and love, the self that God wants one to be. And this duty of charity implies also the humble seeking and acceptance of the help one needs from others to carry on this task.

In the same way, the Christian task of dying to the "old life" of sinfulness and selfishness can take over and transfigure the human task of struggling to grow to human maturity through continual human "dyings." This realization gives new courage and a new incentive to continue this never-ending struggle on the human level—to become not merely a "well adjusted" person, but the person with whom God wishes to communicate for all eternity, the person who can more intelligently and unselfishly minister to others' needs here and now. And it gives full meaning to all ascetic effort to hasten the process of Christian "dying" by such voluntary renunciations as train one to accept inevitable suffering when it comes—because all suffering accepted with Christ can advance, not only one's personal "going over" through death to life, but that of the whole Body of Christ on earth.

These realizations may indeed mean some very practical readjustments in their discoverer's daily pattern of life. In his former way of thinking, the process of self-disciplining and self-perfecting may have seemed to be a matter of choice, of interest only to himself. But now it is seen to be an urgent duty of charity, to matter very much both to God and neighbor. So far as he is free, for instance, to choose one or another kind of work or form of recreation, he now needs to consider the fact that "the thing made makes the maker": whatever he does affects him somehow as a person. It is not a matter of indifference, then, whether or not he chooses forms of work or play that tend to dehumanize, to depersonalize him, or those that tend to make him more fully "himself."

Similarly, to "fast" in one way or another from legitimate forms of self-indulgence may formerly have seemed merely a counsel of perfection outside his scope. But it is now clear that such "fasting," in accordance with the particular demands of his vocation, is a necessity if he is to become what God wants him to be, what his neighbor needs him to be—a purified, re-created instrument of God's love.

SERVING OUR NEIGHBOR IN LOVE

But, obviously, what God wants each of us to become is what He wants everyone else to become—the complete person he is meant to be. Our service to our neighbors, then, must be ordered to helping one another to attain the full "person-hood" God means for each of us. And this means ministering to one another's spiritual, psychic and material needs.

Here again, a great deal of modern thinking is found to echo the Christian message that "no man is an island," that we are responsible for one another whether we are aware of it or not, whether we want to be or not. It has become "existentially" obvious today that the development of each individual person to freedom and maturity is conditioned at every stage by how other people have or have not ministered to his complex physical and psychic needs. It is becoming obvious that the whole of each society and, ultimately, of mankind, is affected by the personal development, or lack of it, in each of the persons making up that society.

And in our age, more than ever before, the potentialities involved in men's use of created things both for good and for evil are becoming intensified and, also, recognized. People are beginning to realize the desperate necessity of sharing the good things of nature and human nature for the benefit of all men, if we are not to destroy one another for them and with them. They are beginning to see the necessity for orienting men's use of their own powers and of material things and forces toward true human welfare—the development of free, fully human persons in a society formed by the cooperation and intercommunication of these persons—rather than towards the perversion of human nature into a servant of technology. And they are coming to realize that, while it is human ingenuity, using material things and forces, that has produced all the marvellous potentialities for the "good life" for everyone, it is human stupidity, selfishness, weakness and ill-will that are frustrating and warping these potentialities.

Today, therefore, it is becoming clear that our Christian work for others: to help one another grow up in all things in Christ, to communicate God's message and love to all men, subsumes and transfigures the human social task: to help one another in society to achieve the fullest and freest personality of which each is capable; freely to share the good things we possess—material things, knowledge, power, know-how, affection—to make a more fully free and human life possible for all mankind; to strive toward the economic, social and political organizations which would more directly promote and foster such a life.

The Word of God certainly does not leave this realization to our own inferences: justice, mercy, kindness to neighbors in the ordinary dealings of social and economic life are inculcated by the whole Law and the prophets as the condition for true worship of God. Christ tells us in the Sermon on the Mount that it is by generosity to everyone that we are to be perfect as our Father in heaven is perfect. He tells us that in serving one another's ordinary human needs we are serving Himself. He tells us that we are to imitate Him in laying down our lives in the service of love.

The temporal order is thus an "end in itself" for Christians, inasmuch as we must be undertaking the human task as such; we cannot bypass it. To the extent that we are concerned with it, we must be working at its various aspects "for themselves," that is, to achieve each as perfectly as possible. The higher and further Christian orientation of human work toward communication with God and with one another in Christ, here and hereafter, must, so far as we are concerned, go through the immediate proper purpose of the work itself. Thus the Christian orientation does not distort, but rather perfects, the human orientation along its own lines, or, rather, it should do so when both are properly understood.

The Christian realizes that the struggle involved in trying to carry out this human task—as in trying to carry out the whole Christian task—is, ultimately, not only a struggle with stubborn nature and human nature, our own and others', but also a warfare with the Evil One and his forces, "the rulers of this world of darkness." He realizes that we have been promised no evident or lasting success in this struggle and this warfare in the present order.

Yet he also knows that Christ has already conquered the Evil One, and that in Christ's Name and in reliance on His love, he too can be victorious, in that he has furthered, in however small a way, Christ's work of taking away from the service of the Evil One both human beings and material things and restoring them to the service of God. The houses we build, the food we raise, the works of art we produce, the institutions and organizations we establish may not endure very long even in human time, and still less do our actions themselves. But the praise they give to God and the praise that they help other people to give Him is caught up into the praise that all creation offers to God through Christ's eternal praise. And the effect of our works and of our actions will endure in the life to come inasmuch as they have helped to fashion the living stones of the eternal "Temple to God in the Spirit," inasmuch as they have helped to make who and what they are the citizens of the eternal City of God.

Christian love of neighbor, then, is found to be something very definite: not some vague good will, or more or less selfish and possessive "do-goodism," but the truly generous love that considers the "who" each of our neighbors is, the love that tries to give to our neighbor as the person he is, that considers our neighbor's needs and tries to care for them, that is open to receiving love and care from him.

And the exercise of this love cannot be a part-time job. It must form and inform everything we do. Striving to put ourselves full-time at the service of this love is not a work of supererogation; it is simply carrying out Christ's *command* to love one another as He has loved us.

In all our contacts and dealings with other people, therefore, we must try to meet the constant human need for recognition as a person. This means the openness to give what is most personal in ourselves to the other persons with whom we come in contact in daily life, and to receive the same from them. It means thoughtful awareness of every other person as a fellow human being and as the particular person he is, in the context of our particular contact or relationship with him—whether he is a salesman at the door, a collaborator in daily work, an intimate friend, a member of one's family. In such communicating, we are communicating Christ's love, in some way beyond our understanding or sensing, and we are communicating in His love, as He is mysteriously present in our neighbor.[3]

Such intercommunication, surely, must be expressed and implemented by what we do. In serving our neighbor's needs, our Lord tells us, we are serving Him. Clearly, therefore, whatever we are doing to serve human needs—whether by work for which we receive a recompense or by one or another work of mercy—we must try to do well, and always try to do better, so as to serve more effectively the

[3] See the chapter "The Sacrament of the Brother," in *Science, Religion and Christianity*.

need it is meant to serve. While Christ certainly accepts our good intentions when we do our best and still serve Him incompetently in our brethren, as Gilson said so cogently, "Piety cannot dispense with technique." And good work, whether in proclaiming the Word of God, in teaching, in any service, in making and distributing goods, should be a shining characteristic of all of us who realize that we are instruments of Christ and that we are serving Christ in serving one another.

But, in the modern context, we need also to examine the work that we are doing, the work that we pay for, the work that we encourage other people to do. For insofar as any work rightly serves a real need—spiritual, psychic, physical—of other persons, insofar as it helps them in its own proper way to live and develop themselves as free human persons, it uses human effort and material things as God meant them to be used, it serves Christ. But insofar as it dehumanizes and depersonalizes men, it is useless and worse than useless, for it serves the purposes of the Evil One.

It is truly terrifying to look at the modern economic and social set-up in this light—such wonderful potentialities for true human living, for the development of free human persons in a free society, and so many depersonalizing and dehumanizing actualities. But, however terrifying, it indicates the present dimensions of our Christian task in striving rightly to serve our neighbor.

Social justice as to wages, hours and working conditions has been the concern of some Catholics for many years, but it is still not the practical concern even of all clerical and religious institutions, let alone of the majority of laymen. And the questions of social justice as to kinds of work and the products of work have only begun to be raised, here and there. Yet, insofar as any specific kind of work is depersonalizing and dehumanizing, it is opposed to the true welfare of the worker. Products and services are opposed to the true welfare of the consumer if they ostensibly serve a need and do not do so, are ostensibly "just as good" without being so, or are calculated to appeal to baser motives and thus encourage subjection to these.

It is, of course, essentially impossible to *force* human beings to become free, mature, "communicating" human persons by any conceivable organization of society. But, obviously, we should be consulting and working with all men of good will, with all the best tendencies in our society, to strive toward the social, economic and educational set-up which would make such development less impossible, less difficult, more appealing to all men all over the world.

Much research and study by specialists are, indeed, needed to disclose the most practicable potentialities in modern society for the truly good life, the truly human life, the life that serves all human needs and not merely material ones. But until each of us begins here and now, by thinking and acting along these lines, to do what we can,[4] many of these potentialities will not even come to light.

And today it seems obvious as never before that unless "the Church"—officially as a visible organization and in the person of her members—in her inevitable economic and social involvement in the world, is seen to be working with all men of good will, and to be working for true human values, personal and social, her proclamation of Christ's message will lack reality and cogency both to her own children and to those outside her fold.

And it must be in this context of personal intercommunication on the human level and consistent effort toward

[4] Sharing thus in the human task is, in a sense, primarily the responsibility of the layman as producer, worker, professional, actively engaged in the temporal order, the life and work of his society. But clergy and religious also, insofar as they *are* engaged in the temporal order, as consumers, employers, and citizens, (and obviously when they are concerned in any production) share to the full the human and Christian responsibility to use rightly human time, energy, talents, and material things, and to work toward a more fully human organization of society.

personal values on the social and economic level, that each of us strives to carry out the explicit communication of Christ's message which accords with his vocation—priests to their flocks, teachers to their students, parents to their children, all of us to those who will hear us. For if we do not show by our actions that we love our neighbor whom we can see, he will hardly believe that we can tell him anything about the love of the God whom he cannot see.

It becomes clear, therefore, that there is no aspect of human life outside the scope of Christian love, outside the scope of the Christian vocation to take part in the work of "re-establishing all things in Christ."

THE MEANING OF SUFFERING

In all these realizations the discoverer begins to see what God wants us to do about all the evils of human life—suffering, mental and physical, frustration, drudgery, death itself. The "offer it up and take an aspirin" approach is not the Christian one. We need first to realize that all these things are evils, they are the effects of original sin and of the sinfulness of mankind. They are the readiest instruments of the Evil One to keep people away from God, from themselves and from one another.

All these evils have, indeed, been transformed by Christ's suffering and death into potential means to His life and to the fullness of life. But they are not these means in themselves. They only become such when they are in some way freely accepted by the sufferer and united with Christ's acceptance of His cross. We do not know, of course, what this "in some way" may mean for those who do not have the use of their freedom or who do not explicitly know Christ. But we do know that it is His suffering and death alone that are life-giving; human suffering and death are fruitful only to the extent to which they are united with His.

For ourselves, then, we need to face the various sufferings that come to us or that we bring upon ourselves. We need to admit to ourselves that each is an evil, and the kind of evil it is, trying neither to minimize it nor to overvalue it. Then we can intelligently undertake to do whatever is possible to remove it or to lessen its effects so that we may continue in our service of God and neighbor. In this context we then must try to accept, with the grace of Christ, the inevitable evils in our lives and to go further along the road of "dying" to our own selfishness and sinfulness by means of voluntary fasting and self-discipline and of "making up what is lacking to the sufferings of Christ for His Body, the Church."

But we cannot force such acceptance on anyone else. It must be the response of each person to what he knows of God, His love, His design. And so, whatever our vocation, we must do everything we can to relieve and do away with these evils as they affect other people; we must try to work toward conditions in which everyone can hear God's message, however it may reach him, and have sufficient freedom to respond to it if he will.

THE MEANING OF CHRISTIAN HOPE

In this perspective, then, it becomes clear that we may need to reorient our whole way of thinking about life, so as not to hold ourselves apart from or try to spare ourselves the wear-and-tear, the daily dying inevitable in any human life fully lived. We need to put ourselves always more fully at the service of Christ's love in every aspect of our lives, striving to accept the various forms of "dying" that this service may involve.

But, as we try to give ourselves, however timidly, to the current of this love, we may find that we are being freed from our resentments against the weariness and "wear-ingness" of our lives. We may begin to see how wonderfully merciful God is to have made all these inevitable conditions of actual human life the means whereby we can come to Him with Christ and help our neighbors to come to Him. And we may find that we are being freed from our despair at our inadequacy, inefficiency and helplessness in the face of others' needs and sufferings. We may begin to learn to suffer with them and to pray for them, rather than suffering uselessly from our own pride and self-interest.

For in all this we can begin to realize the actuality of Christian hope—that it means faith in the reality of God's redeeming and re-creating love, faith that He can and will make each of us the "new man in Christ" He desires us to become, faith that He can and will bring us all in Christ into the eternal current of His life and joy.

Christian hope, therefore, does away with the grimness which so often seems inseparable from "purposeful living," as it also does away with the sentimentality of the Pollyanna type of optimist. To the extent that the life of the Spirit is taking over our lives, even in our weariness and cares we can share in the liberty of the children of God. We can be gaining that freedom of mind which makes truly "liberal" life and action possible. We can become free to delight in what is truly delightful, to praise God for His wonderful works in creation and re-creation, to praise Him for the works He enables men to do. And as we "rejoice in the Lord" ourselves, we shall be communicating this joy to others also.

In this perspective, therefore, the Christian vocation is seen to be fully human, fully actual, and realizable, through God's mercy, in any human way of life. It *is* human life as God enables us to live it with His Son in the Spirit of love, here and now. It is human life oriented toward the perfect life of the City of God, the life of the risen Christ, which He will give in perfect fullness, in the world to come, to all those who have tried to minister to Him here on earth.

CHAPTER 5

The Distribution of Roles

Since, for many centuries, "the Church," practically speaking, meant only the clergy and the religious, a certain amount of overlapping and confusion of roles has inevitably come about. On the one hand, everything "Catholic" had to be planned and executed by a priest, or by a religious who was not a priest when a priest was not available, with a layman called in only as, so to say, a last resort. On the other hand, when a layman became "apostolic-minded," he thought that his contribution must necessarily be along the lines of helping priests or religious with one or another aspect of their work. And when he was overwhelmed with the importance of the "one thing necessary," he considered this to imply that he should live a life patterned after that of monks, Brothers, or Sisters. And all this has meant that many aspects of the work of the whole Church in the world have been more or less neglected, particularly those which of their nature are the task of laymen rather than priests or religious.

Many calls have been issued recently by the highest authorities in the Church, inviting the laity once more to take their proper part in her worship and her work. These calls have had their greatest effect, perhaps, in arousing new interest among priests (and some few of the laity) in the doctrines on which they are based, and so contributing a major share to the emergence of a new outlook on the Christian vocation as such, and on the whole work of the Church. But such calls have not as yet influenced the general attitude to any great extent, because people hear them in the context of the outlook they are used to, as being in the line of appeals for volunteers to give more time in assisting professionals.

It might be thought that such preaching and teaching of the doctrine of the Mystical Body as has been done here and there in recent years—showing the laity that they are members of Christ and so members of one another, each with a responsible function in relation to the life and work of the whole Body—would have changed the prevailing attitude. But this preaching and teaching do not seem to have had much effect. Outside the context of the whole plan of salvation, the figure of the Mystical Body remains a rather distasteful metaphor expressing an abstract idea. Unless people are shown the dynamism of God's design to communicate His love to us and through us, they will take the Mystical Body as just another dogma to be passively accepted along with the rest.

But in the perspective of the plan of salvation, the organic and vital interplay of the roles of clergy, religious and laity in carrying out the whole work of the Church on earth begins to become more evident. In this light, the layman can see the lines of his own special contribution to this work, young people can be shown the realistic bases for a choice of vocation and way of life, and, perhaps, some "redistribution of roles" can take place in work, as it is already taking place in public worship, for the greater effectiveness of the work of the whole Church in her communicating with God and with men.

THE PRIESTLY MINISTRY

The bishops and priests of the Church are those men who have been offered and have accepted a unique kind of cooperation with Christ living and present in His Church. Successors of the Apostles, bishops are sent to other men by Christ as He was sent by the Father, and so they send the priests of the Church (and others whom they may delegate to assist them in various aspects of their ministry).

Bishops and priests, therefore, share in a special way in Christ's work as Mediator—being the mediators of Christ's communicating with men in the holy society of the Church, so as to put each man into direct personal communication with God through Christ, but always in the context of their mediation and their "shepherding."

In the downward movement, so to say, of God's self-revelation and self-giving through Christ in the Church, Christ speaks through them as they proclaim His message to all men. Christ acts through them in the sacraments to communicate the power of His life-giving death to those who receive His message with faith.

In the upward movement of man's response to God, Christ acts through His priests to make His sacrifice present on earth in all times and places, to offer it through their hands, so that all His members may offer it with Him in praise of God, for the salvation of mankind. Bishops and priests order and lead the prayer that Christ's members offer through Him in the community of the Church. And they lead and guide the life of the Christian community through which Christ's communication is to reach out to the whole world.

The work of priests with regard to *themselves* is, then, precisely the same as that of every other Christian: to communicate with God in Christ, to grow in this communication, to cooperate with the work of the Spirit in "passing over" from the old life to the new. Even more than others, they are committed to the personal work of becoming more and more fully "men of God" because of their unique cooperation with Christ in His work of communicating God's love.

But their "ministry" to other men is not some aspect of the ordinary human social task, taken up and transfigured. It is, rather, what makes this taking-up and transfiguration possible. It is what makes possible the taking-up and transfiguration of the personal task of the priest in relation to himself and that of other men in relation to themselves—to become the "christ-ened" person each is meant to be in the life of the Spirit.

It is, therefore, because of the unique sharing of bishops and priests in the one priestly ministry of Christ that all other Christian ministries have meaning and reality, as it is in virtue of the priestly ministry of Christ working through the whole Church that all human life and activity are to find their final meaning and value when Christ returns in His glory to call those who have served Him knowingly and unknowingly to enter the joy of their Lord.

But it is to human persons, in the concrete context of some particular culture and society, that bishops and priests are to communicate the "downward" movement of God's self-revelation and self-giving in Christ, and it is human persons whom they lead and guide in responding to God's love in worship and in life. Their ministry, therefore, includes making this self-revelation and self-giving and this responding through Christ actually available to men—as available as possible, not only with regard to time and space, but with regard to men's understanding and taking hold of God's gift in such a way as to arouse and elicit their own personal response in prayer and life.

So the "sacred sciences" are directly ancillary to the priestly ministry as opening out the Word of God to human understanding from various aspects; so are the arts of human communication, as being the modes of the divine communication and as making possible and facilitating the priest's own task of opening out the Word to his people. And so are the arts of leading men in and to worship and practical Christian living.

Indirectly, at least, all the sciences and arts that open men's minds and hearts to the Light that enlightens every man, and that communicate that Light, may be said to be in some way ancillary to the priestly ministry. And, equally, every human work that helps to free men from the pressure of overwhelming need, that aids them in striving toward full human personality and the truly good life in society, might be said to be ancillary to the priestly ministry also.

The field of the priestly ministry, therefore, cannot be exactly delimited. For it is not in itself some aspect of the common human task taken up and transfigured, yet all the various aspects of that task in some way serve to prepare the way for, or to extend, the work of the priestly ministry and so cannot be excluded from it *a priori*.[1]

Yet the "temporal order," the carrying-out of the human social task, has its own rights and its own proper ends. And a priest can only be "all things to all men" in respect to the flexibility of his charity and skill in mediating God's self-revelation and self-giving to the persons entrusted to him and their response to it. He cannot, any more than anyone else, be thoroughly trained and exercised in several demanding professions.[2] Insofar as he is engaged in carrying on an ordinary human work or profession, he owes it to society—and to Christ—to carry it out on a competent professional level. But the priesthood itself is a profession, in

[1] The priest's function of mediating the response of men to Christ's love in Christian prayer, and of making Christ's sacrifice present in all times and places, might be said to have the aspect of gathering up in his own person and directing through Christ to the Father the self-offering and sufferings of other men as well as his own—the aspect emphasized in the "ministry" of the contemplative priest-religious.

[2] It is obviously of great value to have the disciplines of the sacred sciences and those of some human science fructifying one another in a trained and capable Christian mind and life (which is not the same thing as actually practicing two professions). But there seems no essential reason (other than the tradition of the clergy as being the learned class) why this mind should necessarily be that of a priest, and at least some

the sense of requiring long and special training, special knowledge, special skills and continual growth in exercising them. It is difficult, therefore, to see how, in other than exceptional cases, he can carry out both the priestly ministry and some other profession under modern conditions.

In our times, also, many of the human needs that have been the special concern of priests for many generations —for example, general education and many forms of social work—have become the concern of society itself. And there are Catholic laypeople in increasing numbers in nearly all the professions which might be considered, under one or another aspect, as being indirectly associated with the priestly ministry—teaching, writing and editing, the service professions, and, to a lesser extent, the arts and natural sciences. A considerable proportion of the laity in this country are no longer illiterate and needy immigrants who have to have everything done for them. They are educated, reasonably prosperous, professionally skilled persons, able and willing to serve others, persons whose greatest need is to be shown how they are called to communicate in God's love and how their work and their opportunities can share in carrying out God's plan for mankind.

Moreover, there are only a limited number of priests in the world, a number quite inadequate to carry out the essentially "mediating" work of the priestly ministry and to develop the arts and sciences directly connected therewith. And any vitalization of Catholic life today obviously calls for a great development of the pastoral ministry as such— making the Word of God actually "available" in every sense to people of all kinds, under all kinds of conditions; helping

reasons why the possibility of such cross-fertilization should be made more available to qualified laymen. The special "witness" of a priest-scientist, for example, may be of value in overcoming misconceptions and prejudice, but might not that of competent laymen have its own and more enduring value?

them to open their minds and hearts to receive it; leading and
forming them in Christian worship and prayer; opening out
the full scope of the Christian vocation to them and helping
them to see how to carry it out.

It would seem, therefore, that today it might be at
once more desirable and more possible than it has been for
many centuries to induct qualified laymen as successors to
the priests who are at present engaged in work not directly
connected with the priestly ministry—teaching general sub-
jects, editing publications of more or less general interest,
carrying on specialized forms of social service and administra-
tion, etc. And it also might be both desirable and possible
for priests to call upon qualified laymen, volunteer or professional as indicated, to assist them wherever possible in
many kinds of work immediately associated with the priestly
ministry which do not have to be done by priests[3]—not only
as organists and choir-directors, but as teachers of religion,
lay-readers and leaders, accountants, record-keepers, and so
on—to a far greater extent than has so far been done.

For the priest's unique work of "communicating,"
especially in a parish or analogous context, can be carried
out only by priests. And the more effectively they carry out
their unique task, the sooner will a greater number of the
laity come to understand and live their Christian vocation,
the more fully will Christ's work of worship and of redemption be carried out in our world.

THE RELIGIOUS LIFE

The word "religious," as applied to men and women
living under vows, according to a rule of life approved by

---

[3] The possibilities of restoring the diaconate as a terminal
status and also of officially commissioning laymen as teachers
of religion, as lay-readers and leaders, along the lines of the
Minor Orders as originally conceived, are being much discussed.
See J. Hofinger, *Worship, the Life of the Missions* (Notre Dame
University Press, 1958).

the Church, and as applied to the general form of life they lead, has certainly helped to facilitate various misunderstandings about other ways of Christian life. However clearly one knows that the word refers primarily to the binding of the vows, one can hardly help feeling that neither the diocesan clergy nor laypeople can be as religious, in the general sense of the word, as those who are living the "religious" life. (In the same way, the term "regular" clergy, meaning priests living by a religious *rule*—that is, priests who are also religious—seems to imply that the "secular" or, (far better) the diocesan clergy are somehow less "regular priests" than their religious brethren, however clearly one knows that no such implication is contained in the term itself.)

It may be useful to remind ourselves, therefore, that the characteristic of the religious life in its present form is its commitment, by some form of vows approved by the Church and accepted by a superior in the name of the Church, to a form of life designed to remove the obstacles and facilitate the use of the means to acquiring perfection in the Christian life.

All Christians are bound to practice the virtue of chastity; religious bind themselves by vow to practice this virtue in a special way, by a life of perpetual virginity. All Christians are bound to practice the virtue of poverty—striving, that is, to detach themselves from undue dependence on created things and rightly to use the things they do use. Religious bind themselves by vow to practice this virtue in a special way, by doing without ownership, possession, or control of things. All Christians are bound to be obedient to the holy will of God as expressed in the commandments, the teaching of the Church, the duties and circumstances of their lives. Religious bind themselves by vow to be obedient to a superior in a form of life laid out by their rule and constitutions, to be sure of obeying the will of God rather than their own self-will, even in the details of their daily lives.

Yet the ambiguity of the word "religious" is, in some sense, inevitable in the nature of the Christian life. In the tradition of the Church, the "religious life" essentially implies leaving "the world" in one way or another, to seek God. But the existential world is at once "the world" for which Christ would not pray and "the world" that God so loved as to send His Son to it; and these two aspects are not clearly separable in the present order.

By his baptismal vows, every Christian renounces Satan, the Prince of "the world" (in the first sense); he promises to serve Christ and so help in His work of saving "the world" (in the second sense). Every Christian must continually leave behind, set himself apart from "the world" (in the first sense) in order to help in saving "the world" (in the second sense). Hence, he can never be wholly immersed in the existential world. His orientation is towards "the things that are above," and this is the orientation he must, finally, be trying to communicate to others. Hence every Christian is in some sense leading a "religious" life to the extent that he is leading a fully Christian life. But those who are leading the "religious life," in the technical use of the term, go further. They leave behind, they are set apart from, involvements of the existential world in order to make sure that they will leave behind "the world" of which Satan is the Prince.

Thus by their way of life religious concentrate, as it were, on "dying daily" with Christ in order to live in ever-increasing fullness the life He gives them in the Church, the life of community in His love. By their vows they give up both the pleasures and the distractions involved in family life, in the personal acquisition and owning of property, in the free disposition of their time, strength and talents, in order to be the freer to seek God and to pass over to the fullness of Christ's life.

In so doing, they take part in a special way in Christ's struggle with the Prince of this world. They draw

the whole Church with them into fuller communication with
God in Christ. They communicate God's life to others by
their prayer. They help remove the obstacles to the free
communication of God's love to mankind by "making up
what is wanting to the sufferings of Christ, for His Body,
the Church."

Because they are striving to lead the Christian life
in this way, they are also the better qualified to instruct others
in it, to hand on to others the fruits of their own contemplation. Because of this life of "dying daily" to their human
needs, they are the more free to assist in one or another
aspect of the priestly ministry,[4] or to serve some human need,
without having to receive adequate compensation for what
they do. For they have committed themselves to living inadequately on the human level so as to share more fully in
the sufferings of Christ, to communicate more fully in His
love, and to be the instruments of its communication to others.

In the development of Christian life through the
centuries, in the western Church at least, religious Orders
and congregations have tended to emphasize one or other of
these aspects of the religious life: the contemplatives, the
aspects of prayer and voluntary suffering; those following the
"mixed" life, the handing-on to others of the fruits of contemplation; and the active congregations, the other works of
mercy, corporal and spiritual. Some, if not many, of the
modern congregations came into existence as a result of their
founders' desire to serve some special need as effectively as

---

[4] In the historical development of the Church, it has come
about that many religious are also priests. In other centuries,
monks were often called upon to become priests and bishops,
since they were men who had acquired perfection in the
Christian life and were, therefore, peculiarly suited to the
requirements of the priestly ministry. In later times, men
who already were priests formed themselves into religious
congregations to carry out more effectively, in some particular
historical circumstances, some special aspect of the priestly
ministry. The two vocations may, therefore, be complementary,
but it is obvious that they are not identical.

possible. The men or women concerned realized that to ensure
the stability, depth and permanence of their work, the religious
life was necessary, whereas in early monasticism, many forms
of apostolic work and works of mercy flowed from the religious life as it was already being lived.

But the special witness of the religious life in all its
forms is that it is a willed, a vowed "dying" to the pleasures
and involvements of ordinary human life, in order the more
speedily and completely to attain the life of the heavenly
Kingdom, the life of the Spirit. It witnesses above all, therefore, as does the martyr's death, to the victory of Christ's
love in human beings, enabling them thus freely to lay down
their lives in faith and hope.

This witness is, indeed, greatly needed in our world
today—needed in its full power and beauty. And greatly
needed also are the many works which can be carried out
only, or more effectively, in the context of this witness: the
prayer and suffering of contemplatives, the handing-on to
others of the fruits of contemplation, the giving of expert
guidance in the Christian life, the service of urgent human
needs which otherwise would go uncared for.

Here again, therefore, the special needs and opportunities of our times might seem to indicate that religious
might hand over to qualified laymen the kinds of work in
which it has become difficult to give the special religious
witness under modern conditions or in a given area. Many
needs formerly cared for almost solely by religious are now
being served as part of the general social pattern in this
country, at least in many places. To the extent that this becomes true of any kind of "good work," it may mean that
it is passing over into the sphere of activity proper to laymen,
who are themselves involved in this social pattern. And,
certainly, the less that religious devote themselves to work
that laymen might be doing, the more they will be able to
devote themselves—in this country and all over the world—to

work that they alone can do, where they alone can do it, giving the witness to Christ that they alone can give.

THE VOCATION OF THE LAITY

What has confused much current discussion of the vocation of the laity is, it would seem, the fact that the question has been approached outside the context of the Christian vocation as such. For the "lay" vocation is essentially that to which all the members of the Church are called by the fact of their baptism and confirmation. It is the vocation to which the clergy minister. It is that which the religious carry out in a special form of life ordered to achieving perfection in it.

In one sense, then, the Christian lay life is simply the Christian life undifferentiated. In this sense, it is the vocation to which every Christian should be formed from the cradle, having in itself the potentiality of future differentiation. And in this sense, it is the vocation of all young Christians up to the moment of some definite commitment to a particular form of Christian life.

But it seems clear today that the Christian lay life, as finally chosen or even as "happened into," has its own special witness to give to Christ. The witness of the religious life—however great the variety of forms it has taken and still may take, and however widespread their influence—can never replace, since it is not meant to, the witness of the lay life rightly led. The witness of the religious is needed and so is that of the layman if "the whole is to be leavened."

The fact that the religious life does carry out the one Christian vocation in a more perfect way has led, through the centuries, to many attempts to "religify" the life of the laity along the lines of the religious life properly so called. In part, of course, this has simply meant various attempts to order the lives of zealous laypeople along the lines of the Christian vocation as such—providing due time for prayer and giving direction in the life of prayer, ordering activity to the service of charity. And, obviously, laypeople need all this at any time and in any context. But insofar as such attempts tend to separate the layman from his proper involvement in human society, they may serve to confuse the issue and to hamper the development of lay life along its own proper lines.

It is true that the majority of lay Christians are what might be called the less quick students of the Christian life. They do not have the special glory of the priest and religious, of having given their youth to God—to use the beautiful phrase of Cardinal Lercaro—in one splendid gesture of irrevocable commitment. They are not hastening through the willed "death" of the religious life to the fullness of Christ's life. Instead, they are discovering, through the experiences of ordinary living, the inevitability of suffering, frustration, weariness, and death. But, if they are trying in any way to lead the Christian life, they are discovering in all this the wonder of God's love enabling us to go through all these things with Christ, to learn willingly to accept all this with Him, and so to come with Him to greater fullness of true life.

It is true, also, that laypeople are not, ordinarily, free to devote the main part of their time and strength to direct communication with God in worship and prayer. They cannot seek out suffering by one or another form of fasting to the extent that religious can do so. They can devote only a part, and not the main part, of their time and strength to works of mercy that afford no material recompense; what they do in their working day must, ordinarily, be work that receives a recompense adequate, in the context of their society, to enable them to keep on living and working and to bring up a family.

Yet it is becoming clearer today that it is precisely in this involvement in ordinary human life and work that laypeople can give their special witness to the message and life of Christ. And, as the special purification of the religious life implies daily dying to the pleasures bound up with ordinary living and working, so the special purification of the lay life implies accepting the pain, frustration and confusion of involvement in the life and work of the existential world while struggling against "the world" insofar as Satan is its Prince.

By the continual effort needed to make room in an ordinary life for Christian communication with God in public worship and private prayer, laymen can witness to this communication as the supreme and indispensable focus of human life. By striving to free themselves from the slavery of wants while living under the pressure of real and complex needs and of the wants of others (certainly the special cross of family life today), they can witness to the right ordering of all life—not to comfort and self-indulgence, but to disciplined, mature human living, open to intercommunication with other persons and to the breath of the Spirit. By the struggle to carry out their work and their activities, whether recompensed or not, in the spirit of Christian generosity, they can witness to what all human work is for, both immediately and ultimately, and help to order human life and work toward their true ends.

But they can only carry out this task by being as involved as are their neighbors in the human, social and professional life of their society, being fully "in" the world in one sense, while not "of" it in the other. If all Christians were leading the life of religious, the victory of Christ's love would be apparent indeed, but not within the context of ordinary human life. Thus the special ministry of the layman in relation to his fellow men would seem to be precisely to give this witness to the leaven of Christ's love in an ordinary life, in carrying out some aspect of the ordinary human social task as oriented to its proper immediate ends and to its final end, the building-up of the eternal City of God.

The special "ministry" of the single layperson, in this light, would seem to be more particularly that which he exercises by his work or profession and in relation to it. For in many cases, at least, the single man and woman can devote themselves to their work more fully, in terms of time and energy, than can the married man with a growing family.

And the special "ministry" of married people would, then, seem to be more explicitly twofold: carried out in the husband's work, with its professional and social implications, and carried out in the family and in the interlocking communities and societies of which it is a part. Husband and wife together, as it were, form one complete human entity to carry out this many-sided task, which is that of ordinary human society itself, and in so doing to witness above all to the process whereby God's plan is being carried out, in and through human life and work.

It is not by accident, therefore, that Christian marriage, the sacrament acting, as it were, in the very heart of ordinary human life, is the sacrament that is the image of the union between Christ and His Church. For in Christian marriage, human beings cooperate with God in the whole complex of His creating, redeeming and sanctifying work for mankind, the final purpose of which is the eternal marriage-feast of Christ and His Church, the totality of redeemed mankind.

The Christian laity, therefore, single and married, inextricably involved by the demands of family, professional and community living in the life of their society, witness to the wonderful fact that it is ordinary human life in all its untidiness and unamenableness that God means to transform and transfigure. It is ordinary human persons whom He wishes to bring to the fullness of personality in Christ and to communicate with for all eternity. And His love has arranged it so that through the processes of ordinary human life and work, illuminated and charged with the power of Christ in the life of the Church, human persons can learn what His love means, can communicate in it with Him and with one another, and can communicate it to their neighbors.

VOCATIONAL DIRECTION AND COUNSELLING

Clearly, therefore, the vocations of the priesthood, of the religious life, and of the lay life, single and married, are all necessary for the complete witnessing to the presence and work of Christ in the Church, and for carrying out His work of worship and of re-establishing all things in Himself. Today the particular witness and work of the laity are, perhaps, becoming more clarified than they have been hitherto. And there would now seem to be both a special need and a special possibility of more of the laity becoming aware of their vocation and undertaking to carry it out.

Yet they cannot come to understand it or to live it without the priestly ministry. Priests are needed to make more fully "available" to the laity the self-revelation and self-communication of Christ in the Church, so that they may begin to see it *as* communication, inviting and eliciting their personal response. Priests are needed to open out to the laity the scope of the whole Christian vocation, and of their special vocation, and to study with them the concrete possibilities whereby it may be carried out in one or another context. Priests are needed to form them in Christian worship and prayer, to gather and form them into fully Christian communities, aware of themselves as such, and to lead them as worshippers "in spirit and in truth."

And the laity also need the witness of religious to alert them to the twofold polarization of the Christian life, of the need for prayer in their own lives, of the need for self-restraint, for "fasting," for accepting in obedience the demands and sufferings of their own lives. They need the witness of the religious life, above all, to give them courage, to show them what their own lives, fully lived, also possess and are oriented toward: "Christ in us, our hope of glory."

An "age of the laity," as ours is sometimes called, if it were truly such, would, then, inevitably be an age of the priestly and religious life also. Or, better, it would be an age of the Church, the whole Church, and of the carrying-out of her whole work among men. The more the whole scope of the Christian vocation is made clear, the less difficult will it be for each Christian to find the way in which he himself can best carry it out. The more the whole plan of God becomes basic in our thinking, the clearer it will be how the ways of life in the Church help one another to carry it out. And the more fully every young Christian is made aware of the requirements and the glories of the Christian vocation as such and the more fully he has been formed in it since childhood, the more ready he will be to recognize and accept the demands of the priestly or religious vocation, if he seems to be called to it.

To be sure, not every "cradle Catholic" is going to accept fully his commitment to the Christian vocation, in one form or another, even if he has been made aware of its primary implications since childhood. A continual personal "conversion" and recommitment is needed in any case. And there are always going to be the more or less zealous, the indifferent and the fallen-away. Yet, if the whole Christian vocation begins to be opened out, those who accept it more or less fully and those who refuse it will be able to do so on a realistic basis—because of what it is, not because of what it is not. And those who choose the priesthood or the religious life will be able to do so on a realistic basis also—on the basis of the great need of the Church for priests and for religious, and of a reasonable knowledge of their own fitness for one or another way of Christian life.

Opening out the plan of God, the scope of the Christian vocation, and the place of each way of life in carrying it out, to be fully effective must, of course, be carried out in home life, in education, in parish and Catholic life in general. It must be carried out by a gradual process of leavening, beginning with the already zealous, and so spreading to those who are at present less zealous and indifferent.

But the area in which something could be done immediately is that of vocational direction, guidance and counselling. Young people could be given, in the course of such direction, at least some idea of the scope of the Christian vocation and of the way in which each special vocation carries it out. They could be shown God's plan in a way which would vitalize and reorient whatever religious instruction they had previously received.

They could also be shown, as seems particularly necessary today, something of the inevitability of frustration, pain, weariness, difficulty, and failure in any life. This would help to rid them of their unrealistic delusions about the "easiness" of an uncommitted, not fully Christian life. And it would show them something of what God's mercy means: that He gives us in Christ a life that can transform these inevitable limitations of human existence into means of true life. They could also be shown something of the reality of evil in our world, and of what the Christian struggle involves. For many young people have a real desire for heroic living, *if* they could believe that it would be, not the naive heroism of the "sucker," but a truly realistic heroism operating to some purpose in the real world.

In such a context, then, they could be shown the call to heroism implicit in their vocation as baptized, confirmed Christians, and given as realistic a notion as possible of the special demands, difficulties, and rewards of each of the special vocations and the qualifications that each requires.

At the same time, they could be assisted by all the techniques of modern testing to ascertain as accurately as possible their own special capabilities and weaknesses, in relation to their opportunities, limitations, circumstances.

Thus each young person would, finally, be in as favorable a position as possible to answer the question: In what particular way of life, and special mode of carrying out that life, will I—as I am and as I hope to become—be best able to carry out the Christian vocation, to become the person God wants me to be, to grow in communication with Him here on earth, to enter into His plan and to take my part in carrying it out?

It is certainly true, generally speaking and without taking any number of special circumstances into consideration, that it is the more generous young people who are called to and who choose the priesthood and the religious life. But it serves no good purpose, nor does it ultimately increase the number of true vocations to the priesthood and the religious life, to downgrade the lay Christian life.

On the contrary, only when all the Christian vocations are understood as different ways of carrying out the *one* Christian vocation, when all are seen as different modes of "giving oneself to God," can a valid choice be made. As things are, it happens that many young people feel that the only truly Christian life, the only really religious life, is that of the priest or the "religious." And so, on the one hand, many try out one or the other vocation not suited to them. And, on the other hand, the very many who know that they are not suited for the priesthood or the religious life think that, in consequence, they are not called to lead a fully Christian, a fully religious life at all. Moreover, it is only with the vision of what the Christian life is as it can be led by laymen that the need for the priestly ministry and for the special witness of the religious life can be rightly understood and evaluated.

To continue to give the impression, therefore, that the only life really "led for God" is the priestly or religious life is seriously to weaken the whole Church and to frustrate her carrying-out of her whole work in the world, as the experience of the last centuries certainly shows.

CHAPTER 6

The Orientation of Family Life

The family is, perhaps, the human and the Christian institution which is receiving the most attention today. There exists an almost too abundant literature on its every aspect—so much so that married people tend to feel like the centipede who was asked which leg comes after which and "lay exhausted in a ditch, considering how to run." Yet in the perspective of the plan of salvation, the perspective of the whole Christian vocation, the main lines along which married people might most fruitfully and realistically work begin to stand out afresh, and to form a practical basis whereby to evaluate and put to use advice and teaching on one or another aspect of married and family life.

If the orientation of the Christian life is toward communication with God through Christ in the Church and toward communication with one's fellow men in and for the love of God, this must be the twofold orientation of family life also. The chief—and terrifying—task of married people and parents in family life, therefore, must be not to hinder, but rather to assist one another and their children toward this twofold communication.

This may mean, with regard to the parents themselves, the necessity for growing in self-knowledge. It may mean taking whatever means are indicated to grow in awareness of their own "drives," their own warpings, their own tendencies to over-possessiveness—whatever in their psychological make-up hinders them from being instruments of God's love and not too deceiving images of His fatherhood to their children. Not that any of us can hope to be perfect married persons or parents, but we can take whatever means are available to try to make ourselves, with God's help, less inadequate.[1]

This orientation also means that it is the *personal* communication of each child with God that is most important, something that it is far easier to interfere with than to foster. Yet we know that God Himself is the initiator of such communication, with each human person in turn as with the whole human race. We know that our children have been called to and enabled to enter into communication with God in Christ. So we can pray for its gradual dawning and growth, try not to get in the way of its normal development, and provide our children with the means of fostering it, so far as we can.

With regard to prayer, this would mean ideally some form of family prayer in which the Word of God was communicated and responded to by a prayer containing and formed by that Word—a short reading from Scripture unfolding the plan of salvation in the context of the liturgical year, with the response of personal prayer, and a short psalm, opening out the prayer of praise and thanksgiving and prayer for the needs of others as well as our own.

In many cases, certainly, attempts to set up and keep to such a prayer for the whole family might tend to hinder, rather than promote, each person's own communication with God, however embryonic. It might be possible, instead, for husband and wife to pray together along these lines, possibly using one or the other "Hour" of the various breviaries for the laity now available, and to invite the older children especially to take part.

[1] See Marc Oraison, *Love or Constraint* (New York: Kenedy, 1959).

But the necessity for family prayer is, after all, not of the same order as the necessity for taking part in the communal prayer of the holy Sacrifice, on the one hand, or as the necessity for the prayer "in your room, with the door shut," on the other. When the children are of very different ages, when they have a large amount of formal prayer in school, when scheduling family prayer makes life almost impossible, it might be better, in some cases, to limit formal family prayer to grace at meals[2] and to prayer with the small children, rather than trying to force everyone's praying into the same scheme. In any case, the children's responsibility for their own dawning life of prayer would need to be indicated by example and by occasional word, given on the rare occasions when it would not seem to intrude on the children's rightful privacy.

This orientation would also mean that the direct religious teaching and all the moral training we try to give the children be given in the context of God's plan and of their Christian vocation. This means that whatever religious instruction we give should make use, above all, of God's own means of arousing the children's personal interest. "Bible stories" should, of course, be *stories*, but as soon as possible each should be set in its context in the plan of salvation—the wonderful works of God in the Old and New Testaments being connected with the acts of Christ in the sacraments and so with the children's own life.[3] And moral training should

---

[2] Some families find it possible to include a short Scripture reading at the main family meal, after the main course and before the dessert.

[3] Conversely, it is sometimes possible to provide this living and vital context for the formulations the children are being given in religion classes. But we have to face the fact that, until the catechetical renewal has progressed considerably further than it has, most children will have had their interest dampened by having to learn the formulations too soon and outside of this vital context. We can only do what little we can against: "But the teacher said I have to know this by heart tomorrow."

be aimed at awakening their personal responsibility for what they do, at handing over to them, as soon as they are capable of each new stage, more and more responsibility for themselves and for others.

In this perspective also, one vital aspect of home training is seen to be that concerning the right use of children's own powers, of their time, and of things, as indicated by their natures and by the special purposes they are meant to serve. Today's bias is toward dependence on things and irresponsibility for them. We have, therefore, to do whatever we can to reverse this tendency in ourselves and in our children, to show and to inculcate a truly "aristocratic" independence of possessions and the proper care and use of what we have. For only in this way can the children gain a basic understanding of the nature of Christian poverty and what things are really for: the praise of God and the loving and skillful service of one another.

With regard to the orientation of family life toward true communication with other people, our effort must be not to hinder, but to assist each child through the vital stages of making contact with the world of other persons: with his parents as persons having their own relationship to one another, different from the relationship of each with the child himself; with his brothers and sisters, going through the years from rivalry, envy, competition toward Christian generosity, and so in wider circles of relationship and acquaintanceship.

And here, of course, the children need to be given the means of grasping, from example above all, the orientation of the Christian vocation toward serving one's neighbors in love. This means, for one thing, that both social life and whatever participation is possible for the parents in parish and community projects should be carried out in such a way as not to seem a detriment to family life, but rather its overflowing into the community.

And it means also that in some sense the life of the whole family be ordered—in due proportion, of course, and, as it were, in function of its other purposes—to the husband's dedication and commitment to his own work and its demands. A wife is to be her husband's helpmate precisely so that together they can carry out the whole complex task of Christian married life. Ordinarily, this must mean that she makes her primary, though not exclusive, commitment to her family's life, in such a way that the husband can make his primary, though not exclusive, commitment to his life work.

Our family life, then, must itself bring out the fact that the family is not a self-contained unit, but an organic part of a parish, a community, a society—open to receive from and contribute to the various societies of which it is a part. For the purpose of a family, so far as the children are concerned, is not the static one of simply being a family, but the dynamic one of equipping them, in the context of life itself, for their future lives with God and man, for their own work of cooperating with God and other men to carry out His plan in themselves and in the world. And so far as the parents are concerned, the purpose of family life is equally dynamic—the actual carrying out of their vocation, in its complex and continually changing demands, cooperating with Christ and the Church in furthering the final perfect union of God with redeemed mankind in Christ, of which their marriage is itself the symbol.

CHAPTER 7

Some Implications in Education

RELIGIOUS INSTRUCTION

This is the area where renewal is most necessary, and where it is already under way. Until recently, it seemed as though different and more interesting methods of teaching religion were all that were needed, and religious educators have consequently been infinitely resourceful in working out such methods, with all the assistance of modern visual aids, workbooks, and so on. But it is becoming increasingly clear that the real problem is on another level entirely—that our religious instruction, however ingeniously given, has been teaching children about religion, but has not been oriented toward putting them into personal contact with God's self-revelation and self-giving in the Church in such a way as to arouse their personal response and self-commitment. It has not unfolded to them the plan of salvation in such a way as to bring it home to them and make them responsive to God's invitation to take part in it.

The present catechetical renewal, therefore, is striving to bring about the reorientation and reordering of all religious instruction to achieve these goals. Its aim is to work out and to put into effect a threefold program which would give due place to formal, orderly intellectual instruction, but in due subordination to a biblical-liturgical formation opening out God's design in wider and wider contexts, putting children into contact with the Word of God proclaimed in the Church, training them in Christian prayer formed by that Word, and awakening them to the need for a personal response to God's love in worship and in Christian living.[1]

The danger that such a program might be deficient in exact knowledge of doctrine as formulated by the Church, and so result in mere muddle-headedness about Christian teaching, has already been foreseen. Nobody wants to do away with the formulations of a catechism, but rather to bring them out in their true nature—as formulations designed to prevent misunderstanding and make possible a firmer intellectual grasp of the content of the mysteries[2] of God's self-revealing and self-giving in the Church.

But another danger is that in trying to work out and apply this program more and more widely here in America, we shall yield to the temptation to make realities seem easy by turning them into abstractions that can be memorized, and then to try to make the abstractions seem interesting and attractive by adventitious means. This is the tendency which is, at least in part, responsible for the present state of general education as well as of religious instruction. And it is a temptation which becomes almost overwhelming, unless great care is taken to be constantly on guard against it, whenever there seems to be a question of communicating knowledge, in a limited amount of time, to a large number of persons of different abilities and backgrounds. Yet to

[1] See the chapter "Bible and Liturgy in Catechesis" by F. Coudreau, in *The Liturgy and the Word of God* (Collegeville: Liturgical Press, 1959).

[2] As recent studies have brought out, the word "mystery" in the usage of St. Paul and of Christian tradition (e.g., in referring to the "sacred mysteries" of the holy Sacrifice and the sacraments) means one or another aspect of the plan of salvation, hidden and inaccessible to human wisdom, but revealed and given to us in Christ.

yield to it ultimately frustrates the whole purpose of all education, and *a fortiori* of religious instruction.

For example, as things are now, a ten-year-old may be given the lists of the gifts and fruits of the Holy Spirit and the beatitudes to learn by heart *in vacuo*, not in the living context of their place in Scripture, of the work of the Spirit in the Church and in the child's own life. To help make these lists seem more interesting and learnable, the text may give an ingenious chart picturing the gifts, the fruits and the beatitudes in a kind of family tree, for the child to duplicate or color. Doing so may fix the lists in the child's mind, but still as abstractions, having nothing to do with anything, let alone his life. At least, if later on the child is so fortunate as to discover the living context of these lists, the names may come to life in his mind. But one trembles to think of what might happen if we try to "put over" the plan of salvation and the scope of the Christian vocation without first changing our own mentality about all truth, and especially about Christ's truth. For the point is precisely that it is the truth itself that is truly and intrinsically attractive to us as persons, and it is the truth that sets us free. And truth is, ultimately, not a series of abstract names and definitions, but a Person—Christ Himself.

In an essay called "Is it Possible for a Modern Man to Become a Man of the Bible?"[3] Charles Moeller brings out what all of us need to keep in mind in undertaking any kind of religious instruction at any level. He says that first of all it is necessary for all those undertaking such work themselves fully to believe in the efficacy of the Word of God revealed and given to us in the liturgy and Scripture, and so truly to "proclaim the Word that saves." Next, we need to distinguish among the various kinds of obstacles that keep people away from living contact with this Word, and to remove the unnecessary ones (misunderstandings, textual difficulties, etc.),

---

[3] In *The Liturgy and the Word of God.*

and, thirdly, *to explain the Word of God profoundly, so as to reach man in his fundamental vocation.*

By this, the author does not mean necessarily using long words or complex ideas, though these have their place too. He means, rather, opening out the Word of God in such a way as to awaken the realization that *God* is here speaking to each *person*, as himself, his most personal self, to awaken him to full personality and communication with infinite Wisdom and Love, to awaken him to intelligent, free self-commitment, in the community of the Church, to that divine self-commitment of infinite generosity. This means reverence for the Word of God and for those we are instructing. It means using the inspired analogies, images, "types" of holy Scripture understood in the context of Christian tradition, in preference to any we might think up for ourselves, which so easily tend to the cheap, the trivial, the mechanical.[4] It means true simplicity, the simplicity of Christ Himself.[5]

If all of us concerned with religious instruction in any way—in the home, in the classroom, in the pulpit, in books and articles or texts—try to reorient our thinking and our speaking toward this primary necessity, then the catechetical renewal in our country will be a renewal indeed.

GENERAL EDUCATION

But the religious instruction of children will be suspended in a void, be frustrated and rendered less effective

[4] Fresh analogies, taken from modern science, technology, or anywhere else, are certainly of great use in bringing home philosophical truths—those within the grasp of human reason. But only God Himself and the Church inspired by His Spirit can translate the great realities of His life, and of our life in Him, into human terms. The need, therefore, is not to try to substitute other terms, but to open out the human terms God has given us in holy Scripture in the Church, to open them out to people through the medium of their own human experiences. See my article: "The Psychology of Worship: Another Approach" in *Worship*, June-July, 1960.

[5] See the chapter by F. H. Drinkwater in *Shaping the*

to the extent that the general education they receive does not follow the same lines of personal awakening, of disciplined development in communication with God and men.

Education is receiving almost as much attention today as is family life, and for many of the same reasons: the formation of young people, while primarily the responsibility of their parents, is also the concern of every responsible person in our society; and most thoughtful people feel that there is something deeply unsatisfactory about the effects of what is being done today. Educators themselves are trying to find a way out of the impasse caused by the realization that an education oriented toward adjusting to life, as it has commonly been understood, seems to train young people passively to accept things as they are, making their supreme goal that of "fitting in," while an education oriented toward training the intellect, as it is now being revived, trains only some of the intellectual powers and may still leave the whole person uncultivated and immature.

Without intending in any way to minimize the many and grave problems involved in modern "mass" education, it would seem as if, in the perspective of the human and Christian vocation, we could begin to discern the main lines along which to order our efforts to improve education in Catholic and in secular schools—whether as educators, as parents, or simply as citizens interested in the other persons in their society and in its future.

In the light of this perspective, then, all education needs to be oriented, it would seem, toward assisting embryonic human persons to awaken, develop and discipline all their human powers so as to start or advance them on the road to responsible maturity, and make them capable of further development throughout life. It would be oriented toward communication with God and with men, and therefore toward

Christian Message, ed. by Gerard Sloyan, (New York: Macmillan Co., 1958).

cultivating the sciences and the skills needed for such communication on the spiritual, intellectual, psycho-physical and
material levels. And it would be oriented toward awakening
a sense of responsibility, in the present historical context, for
other men—on the human level, to strive toward the truly
good life for all mankind; on the Christian level, to cooperate
with Christ Himself in carrying out God's plan for mankind.
And it would, therefore, be oriented toward the cultivation of
the sciences and skills needed to carry out this responsibility
as a member of society and a person with some special skill,
able to serve some special need of other persons in society.

Such an education, then, would be centered in the
human "word," human expression in all its forms, by which
we communicate in the wisdom of other men and by which
we communicate with them. It would be an education in
appreciating this "word" and in the skills involved in using it.
The natural sciences would find their rightful place in such
an education as, on the one hand, giving means of communication with the mind of the Creator, and, on the other hand,
means of serving one's fellow men. And the social sciences
would find their rightful place as giving insight into human
nature—one's own and that of others—and of the historical
and social context in which each person is to carry out his
life-work with and for other men, with and for Christ.

In such an education, every course, on every level,
would be given with what might be called a professional
orientation. That is, the aim would be to awaken the student
to the principles involved and to cultivate skill in applying
those principles. Thus the purpose would be not so much to
"teach reading" as to train real readers; not to train children
to "do arithmetic" as to train persons who are to become
arithmeticians, even on the elementary level; not to "teach
science" but to train persons who are at least embryonic
scientists; not to teach "art appreciation" but to train persons
who are artists, even in an inchoate and undeveloped fashion.

Such an education would, therefore, be truly "liberal" in various senses of that much abused word. It would inculcate the general principles which free the mind from bondage to the particular, while inculcating the skills that order the particular in the light of these principles, rather than concentrating on "methods" that train neither mind nor skill. In so doing, it would help to free the individual person, by the development and discipline of his human powers, in communication with the wisdom of the ages, from the limitations of ignorance and from the pressure of immediate needs —opening out to him, even in its elementary stages, the freedom of the wise man, communicating with the wise men of every age including his own, and open to the Wisdom of God.[6]

Such an education would also be truly "vocational," in that it would awaken the sense of the human vocation, and, for the Christian, of the Christian vocation subsuming the human. It would cultivate the knowledge and the skills needed to carry out this vocation in a general way, and this would provide the foundation on which specialization in the knowledge and skills required for one or another profession or type of work might be surely and safely based. Such an education would, therefore, be designed to train and encourage the thinkers, artists, scientists and truly "practical men" for whom there is such great need today, while it would aid in producing a public capable of appreciating and cooperating with the work of these, its wiser and more capable members.

Obviously, the problem is how to make possible such an education, not only for an élite, but for all young

[6] One of the reasons, at least, why many people today find it difficult to "hear" the Word of God in holy Scripture and the liturgy and to make it their own prayer is that our education is so deficient in this respect, so unsuccessful in "humanizing" us. Cultural conditions have changed, it is true. But they have been changing through the centuries, and people in former Christian centuries—even very simple people—experienced no such difficulty; the education they received through *their* culture was apparently more fully human than is ours.

people. And this is the problem we have not as yet really and realistically faced. An education along these lines certainly accords with both the American and the Catholic ideal. It is the kind of education every true teacher would like to be giving, and is trying to give within the limits of the system in which he is working.

But it has seemed to too many parents, and so to too many educators, as though the right of every child in a democracy to an education meant the right of every child to be educated, regardless of his abilities, potentialities or cooperation. And so we have come to have a system of education which, in Mortimer Adler's phrase, enables the students to "cover the ground without having once touched it," without having had their own interest, their own powers truly awakened or engaged. And the existence of such a system has been facilitated by American technical ingenuity and by our ingenuous trust in bigger and more complex buildings, equipment and teaching aids.

It is becoming increasingly evident today that such an education is not "working," that comparatively few young people are being educated by it, and that even fewer are gaining any sense of dedication to anything. The time would seem ripe, therefore, for some real thinking, on the part of everyone, of what education really should try to achieve, and for using all our ingenuity and resources to reorient it toward those goals.

And here it is what the public really wants that finally counts—the general public that votes on questions connected with the public schools, and the Catholic public that also provides both the personnel and the funds for parochial schools. If everyone begins to favor, in whatever ways are open to him, persons rather than things, teachers and students rather than buildings and equipment, if everyone begins to favor the awakening and development of the student's powers, to however infinitesimal a degree, rather than marks that can be precisely charted, we shall begin to work toward an education that will bring out the real potentialities of our young people, and that will do whatever formal education can accomplish to start them on the road to truly human and Christian living, and to trying to make such living possible for all men in our "one world."

CHAPTER 8

A Shift in Emphasis

When the laity are thought of as more or less passive recipients of the Christian teaching, guidance, and means of grace provided by the clergy, then the task of the clergy appears to be that of providing these things and seeing to it that the laity avail themselves of them, at least to the extent sufficient to fulfill their basic Christian duties.

The clergy of our country have, consequently, been providing not only Mass, the sacraments and religious instruction, but also devotions, missions, retreats, religious reading, publications giving the moral guidance and teaching of the Church, etc. And they have been doing a truly remarkable job in making all this available to many people, over a vast territory, and under quickly changing conditions.

In the endeavor to keep people faithful to their Christian duties and to persuade them to use ancillary means toward this end, many motivations have been and are being appealed to: fear of offending God, fear of offending our Lord who suffered so much for us, fear of sin itself, the love of God who is so good, obedience and loyalty to Him and to His Church. These motivations, appealing to sincere faith and devotion, have, certainly, been successful for generations in helping multitudes of people to remain faithful Catholics even under the most difficult circumstances.

Yet today it seems as though, among younger people especially, these motivations are no longer so clear-cut and, therefore, so strong as they were for their parents and grandparents. Many have a vague feeling that since God is so good, He really would not send anyone to hell. Or they feel that the authorities of the Church have to keep on insisting on the moral law, the obligation of Sunday Mass, etc., but that perhaps God doesn't really insist on all this when life is so difficult anyhow. And many, of course, hardly think about their duties at all as soon as they are away from home and home-parish influences.

There is also the appeal to reason and to "faith seeking understanding"—not simply the narrow rationalism of negative apologetics, but the positive approach that indicates the interweaving of faith and reason in the teachings of the Church, their consistency, order and beauty, their fitness and power to order human life to its best ends. This appeal has certainly not been without effect as it has filtered down into the various levels of religious instruction and so reached, to some degree, a considerable proportion of young people. It has had a great deal more effect on the higher levels: in college teaching of sacred doctrine, in classes of "theology for the laity," in books and other publications. But, of course, this appeal is effective only to the extent to which anyone is willing to use his reason. And it loses its effectiveness, even so far as the "intellectual" is concerned, to the extent that life seems unreasonable, essentially disordered, unamenable to reason, even to reason enlightened by faith.

In addition to these appeals, there has been a tendency in this country to try to protect the faithful from influences that might weaken their faith or cause them to lose it. Education, information, health and social services, and various forms of recreation have been provided under Catholic auspices in the effort to keep people away from anti-Catholic influences and propaganda.

In the earlier history of this country, providing many of these services was, certainly, a necessity of charity. Hospitals, schools, and various forms of social service were non-existent in the pioneer days of the Church, and priests and religious went to work to provide them, in many cases for the general public. And in other cases, they set up such services for Catholics because what was being provided by state or private agencies had a definitely anti-Catholic character.

But in our times the situation has changed. Among the needs still served under Catholic auspices, many are being equally well served by state or private agencies, with a sufficient number of Catholics working in them so that the danger of anti-Catholic pressure is at least somewhat lessened. And today it is simply impossible to keep Catholics away from irreligious influences as they go about their living and working. Catholics have become an integral part of their society; they cannot be effectively segregated from the currents flowing through it.

To counter this fact, perhaps, there has been a tendency to go outside the faith itself to find means to make the teaching of the Church and the use of the means of grace seem more attractive. The Church is pointed out as the arch-enemy of Communism, as the bulwark of the home, the mother of arts and sciences. Christian doctrine and the Christian life are inculcated as assuring success in the quest for happiness. Prayer is advocated for obtaining what you want. Charitable giving is urged as being profitable because God will never be outdone in generosity.

All these lines of argument are, of course, based on some truth. And yet this sort of appeal ultimately reverses the whole current of the religious spirit, reducing God to seeming to be the servant of our human needs and desires. It is true that if we seek the Kingdom of God and His justice, all these things will be added. But they will be added only if we seek *first* for the Kingdom—and, finally, only by way of the Cross. "God is the rewarder of them that seek Him," but we must, finally, seek *Him.*

And it is true also that a whole process of purification in the spiritual life is needed to strip us one by one of our various personal, self-seeking motivations so that we may seek God for Himself and not for His gifts. But to authorize and canonize the gift-seeking attitude, as such appeals do, is, in the very name of religion, to hinder people from becoming truly religious.

The difficulty with such appeals is that they are so easy to make, and it is so hard to draw any line. And so the tendency grows to add other benefits to one or the other religious practice—the pilgrimage advertized as a pleasant vacation and a cultural opportunity, the glowing statue that gives a warm feeling of devotion—until all kinds of very tangible benefits are added to the practice of Christian charity by way of raffles, fairs and so on.

These tendencies have come about, certainly, as effects of zeal for souls and their needs. But with the changed situation today and in the light of the new outlook on the whole work of the Church and the nature of the Christian vocation, it would seem as if the time might be ripe for change and reorientation, for new emphases both in Catholic thinking and practice on every level.

For when the Church is seen to be, above all, the holy assembly of persons called to communicate with God in Christ and to cooperate in His plan to extend this communication in themselves and all mankind, it would seem as if the emphasis should be laid on fostering life with Christ in the community of the Church and informed and generous intercommunication with our neighbors—the life in which the living Word present in the Church enlightens and forms His people while redeeming and sanctifying them, so that His love overflows through them into intercommunication with others.

Thus, changing the emphasis in Catholic effort would mean that the motivations of fear of offending God, fear of sin, of obedience and loyalty, would be set in the wider and deeper context of the plan of salvation. It would mean that the appeal to reason and to "faith seeking understanding" be set in the same context at every suitable level of religious instruction.

And it would also mean that the energy, time and resources now spent in providing protective or segregating services for Catholics be used instead, on the one hand, to foster the mature and responsible Christian vitality which is its own best safeguard and, on the other, to serve needs of the whole community in the charity of Christ. It would mean that the energy, ingenuity, time and resources now spent on initiating and implementing various kinds of "extra-benefit" appeals be used instead in opening out the appeal of the Christian vocation itself.

For one of the discoveries of the new outlook is that the holy Sacrifice, the sacraments, Christian prayer, rightly celebrated and participated in, are themselves intrinsically "interesting" in the fullest sense of the term, inexhaustibly enlightening to the simple and to the educated, eliciting and actuating the response and self-commitment of the participants.[1]

The first effort, therefore, and one that is already being made in many places, would be toward the meaningful celebration of the holy Sacrifice, particularly of the Sunday

[1] Such an approach might be thought far too idealistic were it not for the fact that it is being carried out effectively in the very difficult circumstances of the Catholic "diaspora" in East Germany behind the Iron Curtain. It is true that the core of the faithful concerned were an élite already tried by previous persecutions. But perhaps our many advantages in this country could compensate, if one may put it that way, for the lack of persecution. See "The Liturgy and the Word of God in Parish Life in the German Diaspora," by Most Rev. Otto Spülbeck, in The Liturgy and the Word of God.

Sacrifice. This doubtlessly involves a many-sided effort to bring out, by the celebration itself and by the sermon, who God is, who His Son is, who the Spirit is in whom we worship. It involves the effort to make it a celebration that will elicit the true active participation of all present in receiving Christ's word and life, in responding to God's love with Christ as a member of the Christian community, in praise and self-offering with Christ to carry out the Christian vocation.[2]

And the same kind of effort would be directed toward making baptisms, marriages, funerals (and wakes), confession, confirmations become celebrations designed to awaken and inform the faith of all present, from one or another aspect, and to arouse their commitment to the whole Christian vocation.[3]

A growing body of literature is available giving suggestions both as to the "why" and the "how" of efforts directed toward such celebrations—for priests, and for the people, on various levels—and there is no need to try to summarize them here. But perhaps the purpose of such efforts might be stressed, for when it is lost sight of, "active participation" becomes a mere external formality, another "gimmick." The purpose is not simply to substitute one system or way of doing things for another, but to open out to the

---

[2] The need is, obviously, not only "to bring the people to the Mass," but to bring "the Mass to the people" (and so with the celebration of the sacraments, etc.). And this brings up many questions as to the adaptation of the liturgy in order to bring out its essential lines and facilitate true participation —questions which have been under discussion by experts, encouraged by the Holy See, for many years. But until everything possible is done to bring the people and the liturgy together under present circumstances, and, above all, to change their mentality about the holy Sacrifice and the sacraments, such adaptation would lack full effectiveness. In any case, helping to change this mentality is a task we can all share in, while adapting the liturgical rites is the task, finally, of the Holy See itself.

[3] J. Hofinger, *Worship, the Life of the Missions* (Notre Dame University Press, 1958) gives many suggestions to stir the pastoral imagination.

people *Christ's* speaking and acting in the community of the Church, to draw them into *Christ's* response to the Father in the Spirit of love.

Such efforts, to be fruitful and effective, need to be made in the context of an over-all effort to open out holy Scripture as the record of the "common experience of God and mankind,"[4] the liturgy as the continuation of that same experience here and now in one mode, and the Christian life as its continuation in another, all oriented to the final carrying-out of God's design.

For it is only in this light that Scripture, the liturgy, and the Christian life begin to explain one another so that the people can begin to hear the Word of God speaking to them and giving Himself to them in the sacraments and the holy Sacrifice. It is only in this light that they will begin to realize, in the vital way intended by God and implicit in the liturgy, the reality, the vitality, and the scope of their Christian vocation.[5]

This over-all effort to open out the liturgy, Scripture, and the Christian life in their dynamic relationship to one another must, of course, be undertaken in direct connection with the celebration of the holy Sacrifice and of the sacra-

---

[4] Louis Bouyer in *The Meaning of Sacred Scripture* (Notre Dame University Press, 1957).

[5] The inauguration of "liturgical" practices and instruction on the parish level and elsewhere has, certainly, in the past often failed to engage more than a limited few of the faithful. This is due to the fact that those concerned in the liturgical movement have themselves been discovering through the years the full scope of the outlook of which "social worship" and the idea of sacramentalizing life are aspects but not the whole. These aspects are, of course, valid in themselves, but they lack full reality and cogency outside the context of the whole plan of salvation. It is now becoming clearer that everything must begin with God's initiative, speaking and acting through His Word in the Church to carry out His plan, and that, consequently, the communicative nature of Christian worship and Christian living and their dynamic, historic orientation must form the basic lines of effective efforts for the renewal of worship and life.

ments. But this needs to be supplemented in every possible way, on every available occasion. The meetings of parish societies, Lenten and other extra services, missions, study-clubs, Communion breakfasts and the like might furnish varied opportunities.

And in taking such opportunities, the meaningful devotions of the present day could be made pivotal, as it were. Devotion to the Sacred Heart could be shown as finding its full meaning in the context of the plan of salvation, as the encyclicals on this devotion amply indicate. The various forms of devotion to the holy Eucharist might be shown as ordered toward participation in the Eucharistic Sacrifice and as being, like the Sacrifice itself, an anticipation of the life of the heavenly Kingdom with which we are united in a special way through the sacramental presence of our risen Lord.

Devotion to the holy Mother of God could be shown to be, not a kind of supernatural "momism," but devotion to the human person who perfectly cooperated in God's design, who perfectly received the Word in faith and responded to it, the perfect Christian, type of the Church and our Mother. And praying her Rosary could be shown to be meditative prayer on God's design, as Mary herself took part in that design with her Son, as it was fulfilled in her, and as it is to be fulfilled in and through us.[6]

In ways like these, people would not be made to feel that they were being given something strange and different from their "old-time religion," but, rather, that they were being aided to realize its full scope.

But such efforts toward fuller communication of the people with Christ in the holy Sacrifice, the sacraments and prayer—that is, the carrying-out of their Christian vocation in worship—need to be complemented by carrying out this vocation in parish and other activities, if the laity are to realize its scope and to carry it out in their own lives.

[6] See Bouyer, *Introduction to the Spiritual Life.*

A primary necessity here is that the priest himself be convinced of the reality of the Christian vocation of his people. If he thinks of "active participation" as just another kind of prod to unwilling children or just another sop to the spirit of activism, and if he calls upon his people for aid only or mainly in raising money and in "putting on" fairs, raffles, etc., he will never get them nearer to a realization of their Christian dignity and responsibilities. But when he calls upon them for aid mainly in carrying out the worship of the Christian community, in teaching Christian doctrine, and in "works of mercy," then he shows, more convincingly than in words, that he recognizes his parishioners as mature, responsible, fully initiated members of the Church. And he also shows thereby that the parish is primarily the assembly of the holy people of God, called to worship and to "doing the truth in love," rather than a social grouping in the ordinary human sense.

Beyond this, as the people begin to see more of the implications of the Christian vocation they could be helped toward further realizations of what it implies, very practically, in relation to parish gatherings, in relation to money-raising projects, and in relation to cooperation in community activities and projects.

Parish gatherings, for example, whether general or of special groups, are for the purposes of furthering the members' knowledge and awareness of their Christian vocation, for discussing practical applications, for planning and undertaking the necessary work of the parish, and for having a good time enjoying one another's society in the bond of Christian love.

But to use such gatherings to "make" money is to waste a great deal of time, energy and effort in making simple Christian generosity difficult, if not impossible. Of course, when this is done, the already generous are actually twice so—in putting on and carrying out the money-raising projects and in taking part in them also. But once people begin to see how much simpler it is just to give whatever is needed,[7] they might begin to give the simpler way a good try. And once they begin to realize that "giving to God" on the chance of acquiring a Cadillac is not really giving at all, it might slowly become evident that it would be better not to have the money or the things the money would buy if it has to be raised by such means. And when the time, energy and resources once spent on raising money became available for other projects, new possibilities might begin to open out— possibilities of caring for further needs in the parish and the community, whether as a parish organization, or by joining in community projects, or by personal initiative.

Clearly, efforts such as these, both in relation to worship and to parish activities, will reach mainly already-practicing Catholics, and to the extent that they *are* practicing and taking part in services and activities. But such efforts *would* reach these people. And the increased vitality of their Christian worship and Christian living might then begin to attract the less zealous, and so on out to the luke-warm and the indifferent. And finally, perhaps, at least some of those would be reached who never before had been aware of whom they were rejecting, never having been able to find Him in what they saw of the Church and their Catholic neighbors. At any rate, it is hard to see how anything could be lost by making this attempt.

There is no need to blueprint what this change in emphasis toward vitality of life in the Church, on the one hand, and toward intercommunication with our neighbors, on the other, might imply, beyond what has been said already, in wider diocesan and national contexts.

[7] Various plans for "tithing," that is, for planning to give a certain percentage of one's income (not a full tenth, considering today's taxes, but something like five percent divided between parish and other needs) have been worked out and are being used in many places.

If all the effort now spent on "extra benefit" appeals were reoriented toward opening out the reality and the wonder of the Christian vocation....[8]

And if, without losing any of the variety that should always characterize Catholic life, all the resources and energy now dedicated to "promoting" various devotions and exercises of piety were dedicated to opening out in these same devotions and exercises the full scope of God's design, the various aspects of the Christian vocation....

And if, without losing the freedom of initiative and activity that should also characterize Catholic life, an evaluation were made of the various services offered under Catholic auspices, to the ends that: those which serve a human need otherwise not cared for were extended to the whole human group or community, if this is not already the case; those that serve a need adequately cared for under other auspices were reoriented to some need not as yet served, whether of Catholics or of the whole group or community; and only those were retained that could be carried out with reasonable effectiveness....not to speak of taking every opportunity to work with those of other faiths, or those of none, to promote human understanding and human welfare....

If these and similar "ifs" began to be realized, if the change of emphasis here sketched out began to be made,

---

[8] When everything has been said about the social and cultural reasons for the cheap, sentimental or mechanically "tasteful" ways in which the realities of the faith are, more often than not, incarnated in Catholic writing, music, art, architecture and so on—with the best intentions, derogating from God's majesty and distorting people's understanding of these realities—it would seem as though the basic reason were a desire to make them seem attractive even by associating them with cheap emotions and self-interest. Only with the growing realization of the true vitality and attractiveness of the Christian life, of God's plan and of the Christian vocation will Catholic art generally be renewed. But also, whenever *any* worthy art replaces unworthy, it aids most powerfully in fostering these realizations. The responsibility of all patrons here is, therefore, very great, as is that of every Catholic artist in any field.

people would still be sinful, still subject to weakness, temptation, ignorance, still liable to mistakes and misunderstandings. There would still be innumerable problems and difficulties facing the Church and her zealous members—perhaps more problems and more difficulties. But they would be the real problems and the real difficulties inherent in the life of the Church and her members here on earth in carrying out their task in human history. They would not be the unnecessary and sterile problems created by our taking the Church and the Christian life for something other than what they are.

The appeal of what the Church really is—the Bride and Body of Christ, the People of God, the Kingdom and City of God, the Temple being built to Him in the Spirit; the appeal of her life as our communication in God's life; the appeal of her charity as the communication by herself and her members of Christ's infinite generosity—these are the only appeals that are ultimately effective, in a pluralist society or any other, in carrying out Christ's work: to draw all things to Himself, to make all men one in Him to the praise of the Father in the love of the Spirit.

"I have come to cast fire on the earth, and what will I but that it be enkindled!"

Postscript

All of us tend, of course, to spend considerable time in discussing what "they" could do and should do, especially the "they" who hold any kind of authority that we do not. But in bringing about any reorientation of Catholic mentality and practice, such as seems indicated in our times, even the highest authorities in the Church or the diocese or the parish can accomplish very little unless all of us who see anything of the issues involved do what we can to reorient our own thinking and ways of acting, and to influence the thinking and acting of those immediately associated with us. For any such reorientation must take place, not by instant change, but by a gradual leavening. It is only in the hope of aiding, in some small way, the working of the leaven that I have ventured to write this book.